Cakes, Bakes and Business

the practical guide to starting your home baking enterprise

Britt Whyatt

D0166553

Published in Great Britain in 2017 Under the
HypnoArts label by
the Academy of Hypnotic Arts Ltd.
1 Emperor Way, Exeter, EX13QS
Tel: +44 1392 314090
HypnoArts.com

Enquiries should be addressed to

HypnoArts Publishing
bookpub@hypnoarts.com

First printed edition 2017
British Library Cataloguing in Publication Data
ISBN: 978-0-9547098-9-1

Dedication

For Tim, my everything.
You, me & the sea.
In memory of my loving mum,
who made me the woman I am today.

Contents

Where To Start

How do I start a cake decorating business from home?

It's up there with the top 5 questions I get asked regularly. I wanted to take some time and address this properly and tell you just how I started mine, from the very beginning. This book is a useful and practical guide on what you need to do to start your new delicious venture.

My name is Britt and I run a multi-award-winning business and baking blog called 'She Who Bakes'. It's a baking resource website full of recipes, tutorials, articles and advice.

These days, I concentrate on teaching others how to bake and decorate cakes via my online classes and social media pages but for many years I ran a successful cake decorating business from home. I made cakes for all occasions and by the time I closed my order book for good in 2015 to concentrate on other parts of my business, I had been part of hundreds of customer's life events. It's a fantastic feeling.

I never actually wanted to bake cakes for a living, it wasn't a burning desire, family business or entrepreneurial spirit that spurred me to kick start a new career. For me, it was simply an enjoyable hobby mixed with redundancy.

I started baking and decorating cakes in 2010. Having never really baked before, and being at home recovering from surgery and the after effects of septicaemia, as well as dealing with severe depression and social anxiety after the loss of my single parent mum when I was just 16, I was asked by a friend to make a cake for a charity bake sale.

I had no idea what I was doing when I said yes!

I think the extent of my baking adventures up until then had ended with the one time I made butterfly fairy cakes with my late nan when I was about 7 years old, and they were burnt when I accidentally turned the oven up (sorry nan).

So, for this I bought a packet mix, an inadequate amount of icing and created a square shaped Pudsey cake. (He's a little yellow bear and the mascot for a British charity, Children in Need.) I should point out as well, he has a round face, not a square one! But I worked with what I had at the time; a square roasting dish.

He was cracked and creased, overcooked and under-baked all at the same time. He looked and tasted awful but making him had made me ridiculously happy during a time when happiness was scarce for me.

Baking gave me such a wonderful feeling, a sense of purpose and joy I hadn't had in a very long time. I fully stand by my thoughts that baking saved my life. I was in such a terrible place and seven years later I have completely come out the other side.

All thanks to that little, square, under-baked, slightly burnt, cracked Pudsey cake.

I don't think you ever forget your first cake. I really enjoyed the process of creating him and quickly fell in love with baking and the feeling it gave me. I went on to make a few more cakes over the following weeks, (30 in the first month or so I recall...), when a friend asked if I would do him a favour and bake a simple cake for his birthday party, I was attending, as he had been let down last minute by his Aunt.

Panic suddenly set in. I was ridiculously nervous because if I baked at home for me and something went wrong, it didn't matter, it would still be eaten and I would put it down to a learning experience. All at once there was added pressure.

What if he didn't like it?

What if his friends laughed at it?

What if no one wanted to eat it?

The negative thoughts were relentless. But, I put on my big girl pants, took a deep breath and got to work. I finished the cake and despite it being far from perfect, I was delighted to see how happy my friend was. It was through that party I had a few enquiries, then because of the photos I had posted online I had a few more messages. After that I began to wonder if I had found my new calling!

I got the necessary certification I needed, my food health and safety qualifications, I got my kitchen checked over and was given my 'star rating', (don't panic, more on this later in the book!) and I was seriously considering starting a proper business.

A month later I was unexpectedly made redundant and it appeared the choice was made for me! I created a business Facebook page and started to get the word out that I was taking cake orders.

It didn't take too long for my first commissions to come in and then suddenly, I was a professional cake maker!

One thing I did notice however when I was setting up my business was a lot of conflicting advice available online and nothing that went into too much detail on the 'how' to set-up. More just 'do this then that' without explaining too far into it.

That is how this book was born.

What started as a rather lengthy blog post grew and evolved into something much more. A quick 'I'll just write that' idea morphed into the book you see before you (not without its own challenges I assure you!). Massive thank you to both Tim and Jemma for helping me realise this was more than just another blog post.

If you've bought this book for yourself, I'm guessing you've been baking for a little while, covered yourself in flour more than once, spent far too much money on cute baking tools and novelty tins that were on sale, that you'll probably never use (or is that just me...); you've been making cakes for family and friends at gatherings and birthdays and the reception has been positive and you've been enjoying creating. So, through requests from people in your life, or a desire for a career change, whether voluntary or enforced, or a little spark of entrepreneurship and wanting to be your own boss. The life of a professional cake maker is calling you.

Most of my baker friends who I speak to, admit that, like me, they fell into cake decorating by accident and starting a business seemed like the next logical step. From picking up a bowl and giving it a go and not being able to put the bowl down, to starting a family and wanting to bake cakes for their children and be the coolest mum on the playground, to being made redundant and wanting to do something completely different, turning your beloved hobby to your career can be a very rewarding thing to do.

However, you should be aware it's not without its difficulties. Difficulties that you may not think of at the start when you are on a sugar high. You will face obstacles in this line of work just like any other profession. A big challenge you will face is trying to find a good work/life balance.

Self-employment can be tricky if you're not prepared.

You can't just leave your work behind you in the office at 5pm and go home and forget about it.

Your work will be all around you. Your weekends may change as Saturdays are the most popular days for cake orders being collected/delivered; I used to have my weekend on a Sunday & Monday instead. Making time for yourself and your family is so important and is easy to forget. You fall into the trap of thinking that because you will be home more, (if leaving outside employment to start up), that you will be 'around' more. This is usually not the case.

Making cakes for other people sometimes means you will be working in the kitchen until very late and if you're not careful the time will seem to fly by. This has happened to me on more than one occasion! I've been sat making sugar buttons, listening to music and drinking coffee and before I knew it, it was past midnight! Once, I had a friend who thought I sat at home and watched TV all day (I mean, the TV is usually on in the background…), occasionally making the odd cupcake and doing a bit of washing up.

It was only when she came round for the day and she saw me running around the kitchen at full speed in a whirl of icing sugar, stressing about fondant ducks and having enough butter in the fridge, that she realised my job was a lot harder than she originally thought.

You should always make time for the important things, especially if your new office is your home.

Customer service and public relations may be a tricky one too. Running your own business means the buck stops with you and you must be the one to cover yourself.

You will be dealing with people and be an integral part to their treasured occasions and future memories. During their birthdays, weddings, christenings and other occasions, your work will be part of their special day forever. Their event should be as important to you as if it were your event. Often there were times when I would be sad that a cake was getting collected because it felt like I had put a piece of my heart into their work, and I was so proud, I wanted it to remain in my kitchen forever. You get attached to these things! It's more than just cake.

You will need to learn how to deal with tricky customers, especially if you've not had experience in a customer service role before. You will need to learn what to do to cover yourself should the worst happen. This is so important. We go over all of this, in the 'Dealing with Customers' chapter. I've also included a sample cake contract as well as terms & conditions at the end of the book for you to use and to customise. Feel free to add, take away or amend any details you like. Your contract reflects your business and your needs.

Also at the end of this book, for added security and peace of mind for yourself, and your business, I have included a sample collection and delivery disclaimer form template. This can also be rewritten to suit your needs. This ensures the customer confirms the cake they have ordered, is the cake they receive or collect. The last thing you want is a customer asking for a refund two days after the event and you have no proof they said it was ok. Luckily, this never happened to me in my business, but I have seen it happen and it can get quite unpleasant to deal with. As I say, (and will say over, and over again, in this book), it's best to cover yourself and better to be safe than sorry.

Pricing your work is one of the biggest challenges when you're running your own business. For the first year or so I was in business I MASSIVELY undercharged, to the point where I was spending more on equipment and ingredients than I was making from selling cakes.

This is such an easy trap to fall into when you make a career from your hobby. You don't see the newest cake gadget as a business expense, not at the start, you see it as something fun to buy and play with, which of course it is! However, if you treat everything you buy as a 'treat for your hobby' rather than an 'important tool for your business', you're going to lose out. You must make sure you are charging enough for your hard work to make your business viable, otherwise you may as well just keep it as a hobby. If you aren't being paid properly for the work you do, there's a chance you will start to resent it and feel under appreciated.

Charging for bespoke, handmade products where one of the biggest components is your time can be daunting and uncomfortable at the start. You will almost certainly undercharge in the beginning. I've written lots of handy tips in the 'How Much Should I Charge?' chapter as well as pricing advice for wedding cakes in that corresponding chapter also.

There's a helpful template at the end of this book for working out your cake costs. I used these, every time I made a cake. I have completed the form for you using an example cake and given you a blank sheet to copy and fill in for your orders. This will help you know exactly how much your cake will cost you to make, and you can then calculate how much your profit margin will be.

This was a lifesaver for me. I would estimate a cake would cost me £22 to make, for example, but when I worked it out it cost over £30! That may not seem much of a difference, but if I underestimated every single cake I made by that much, the losses would soon add up.

I've also included an accounts template to keep track of how much you are spending on your business and I go a little more in depth about accounts and self-employment later.

I think one of the most important things you need to know before embarking on a new cake decorating career is that it isn't easy. Making cakes is the fun bit, but know this isn't where you will be spending all, of your time. Admin, marketing, shopping, cleaning; these tasks will all be part of your job as well.

You need to have a solid love for baking and cake decorating and making cakes for other people or it simply won't be worth it.

Just like starting any other business, you need to make sure you have the correct tools in place to fulfil your customer's requirements. I don't just mean the tools you'll find in your kitchen cupboards and drawers, either, although they will take over any available space you have! I mean the drive, determination, will, and above all, passion.

There will be long days and longer nights.

There will be stress and pressure not just from yourself but expectant wedding couples and birthday parties.

There will be times you will want to throw your mixer out of the window and you will never want to see another cake again for as long as you live.

There will be baking and re-baking.

There will be hours of lining tins and a mountain of washing up, that never seems to diminish, whenever you get creative.

There will be invoicing and accounts, emails and marketing and a whole host of admin that falls to you.

There will be ups and downs.

There will be rejections and knock backs. There will be cakes that make you cry, both for good and bad reasons.

There will be negativity thrown at you from different sides.

There will be times you wonder if you're cut out for running your own business after all, (this one crept up on me so many times). The baking and cake decorating career path isn't always sweetness and light.

But if none of that puts you off, and if you truly love making cake, then the life of a professional baker may well be for you!

There are a few practical elements you will need to put into place before taking orders from the public. Over the chapters of this book, I will be showing you how I started up my multi award-winning business, 'She Who Bakes' and how you can put into practice the advice I have based on my experiences.

Best of luck with your new business and happy baking!

Your Kitchen

Your kitchen is undoubtedly the single most important room in your cake business. I didn't have a kitchen of my own to use when I first started baking. I baked my first few cakes at my friend's house and I would keep my tins and cake equipment in an old picnic basket in her conservatory!

I will always be grateful to Sue for not only letting me store everything there and making a mess of her kitchen regularly (including blocking her sink once or twice, sorry!) but also for being the one to task me with making the Pudsey charity cake in the first place! If that conversation had never happened, I wouldn't be here writing this book today.

When I finally moved into my own kitchen, it felt like I had so much space and storage compared to where I started!

The joy of empty cupboards!

This quickly got filled up with gifts and gadgets, equipment and tins and before I knew it, there was no room for any actual pots, pans and kitchenware!

I made a note of how much space I *actually* had and how much space I *could* have, if I played a bit of kitchen Tetris. If I moved the slow cooker into a different cupboard and stacked the pots and pans properly, I was left with valuable space. Have a good look at your kitchen and see what you can do. The biggest business can be born from the smallest space. Remember, the likes of Apple, Google and even Walt Disney all started from a humble garage!

When I moved in with my partner Tim, the kitchen set up left a lot to be desired. The floor was uneven stone, and on two levels, there was a small fridge just big enough for a packet of butter (maybe a slight exaggeration), there was a free standing old gas oven that didn't look like it had been used since 1941 and the sink was seemingly floating on four wooden legs with a large empty space underneath it. Thankfully it doesn't look like that now!

There will always be a way to make your kitchen work for you and as with anything you need to look at it practically. Do you have enough worktop space to roll out icing and stack cakes or will you need to buy a separate table for your decorating? Do you have the storage space already needed for tools and equipment or will you need to buy a separate unit? What tools do you currently have? It's easy to get caught up in the 'buying new stuff' cloud but there's little point in buying something you've already got or won't use.

Something I wish I knew when I first started is, it's important to have somewhere to sit. I know when I am icing cakes and decorating them I'm usually standing but when you're spending hours making little models and decorations out of sugar, leaning over the whole time can be bad for your back.

I didn't have anywhere to sit in my kitchen and got a frozen shoulder once from spending too long hunched over when I was standing. The painkillers I had really spaced me out and put me back for a week. After that, I made sure I had a comfy seat and a good height worktop to sit under and it really made the world of difference!

Kitchen Logistics

So, you've looked around your kitchen, organised your cupboards and drawers, bought a storage unit for all your cutters and moulds and you're pretty sure your worktop will be big enough for an extravagant wedding cake. What now? Well now we move onto the legalities of working from your home kitchen.

Contrary to popular belief, you can't just wipe down your kitchen, buy a mixer and set up a sign saying, '*Cake Shop*' and start trading. There are a few things you need to put into place before you can start taking money from customers and making cakes as a business. These steps might not seem important, but

I promise you, they really are. Not just from a *health and safety* standpoint, but a legal one too.

If you're renting your property, you must get permission from your landlord or housing association before starting any business. It is best to *get this in writing*, either in a letter or in an email as you may need to show this to your local council when you speak to them and it's good to have for your own business records. **Please be aware, they can say no.** They own the building and they are entitled to object to any commercial ventures. That said, in 2015 the Small Business, Enterprise and Employment Act was introduced, giving tenants the right to work from residential properties, provided the property remains a residence first and foremost (so no more than 40% of it should be used for commercial purposes), and that the landlord has given their permission for the property to be used as such.

However, a landlord cannot withhold permission to run a business without 'reasonable' justification. These include;

Nuisance to neighbours. This could be anything from loud noise, increased footfall to the property or late-night hours of operation: if you haven't got your food mixer on at 1am and you don't have 20 people all collecting cakes at once, I'm pretty sure you'll be ok on this one.

Excessive wear and tear (or if the nature of your work might diminish the condition of the property). This one, I believe is aimed at home businesses such as child minding or pet-sitting services that may not be kind to walls and soft home furnishings, especially if the property came with furniture that you must return at the end of your tenancy. That said, with a cake business, most of your work will be done in the kitchen and if this is kept clean and tidy I can't see it being a problem.

Change in mortgage. If you are using too much floor space of the property for work, the property may be deemed '*commercial*' rather than '*residential*' resulting in the owner being in breach of the terms and conditions of their mortgage agreement.

Usually, a friendly conversation with the landlord should settle any of these concerns. Cake businesses are generally seen as a 'low risk' business and if you are open and honest about what you plan to do, and explain that none of the reasons above come into play, there shouldn't be much of a problem. That said, if you have the conversation and your landlord continues to refuse your request to run a home business without good reason, contacting your local council or citizens advice would be your best move. But it hopefully shouldn't come to that.

Do make sure you tell them, however. As with everything in life, it is a lot easier to get something settled with communication. The last thing you want is for your new venture to land you in legal hot water.

Then *you **must*** register your kitchen as a food business with your local council. What this means is that you inform your local council or local authority that you intend to set up a food business. It doesn't matter if you're making one cake a month or 10 cakes a day, this is something you MUST DO. This process is the same for most types of food businesses including catering businesses run from home and mobile or temporary premises, such as stalls and vans. Put simply, it's *mega important*.

Why is it such a must? Well it all comes down to keeping people safe. As you will be selling your products you have a duty of care to your customers to ensure the cakes they are buying from you, are safe to eat. Now, this all sounds very extreme, I mean why wouldn't the cakes be safe? But even though a cake business is a 'low risk' one, it is still a legal requirement that environmental health come and inspect your kitchen to see if it is *'fit for purpose'*.

It doesn't cost you anything to register (bonus) and your registration can't be refused. However, if you are caught trading from a kitchen that isn't registered, you risk being fined a hefty amount or worst case can be imprisoned for up to 2 years. This isn't said to scare you. Registering your premises doesn't take very long, is **free** and is well worth doing.

You *must* register your premises with the environmental health service at your local authority, at least 28 days before starting to trade (so before you start charging money for your bakes). If you're in the UK you can apply for the licence on the **gov.uk** website.

Once you've filled in the online forms and registered your kitchen, your local authority will be in touch to arrange a time for an environmental health inspector to come and check out your kitchen. They will usually offer you an appointment in a couple of weeks, depending on their workload, so please don't worry about getting a phone call saying they will be coming to visit that afternoon and going into a panic (I was guilty of this!).

They are usually very nice people who on visiting you will give your kitchen a hygiene rating out of 5. They will be checking your business to ensure it meets the requirements of food hygiene law. *It all sounds very intimidating but they are there to help.* You can call them in advance and ask for advice if you're unsure of anything before they come to your house.

So, what is a food safety officer looking for? Some things include;

How hygienically the food is handled and stored. Where your ingredients are kept, where you are planning to decorate your cakes and where you are planning to store them ready for delivery or collection. Make sure you have a specific safe place to keep them once they are boxed up. So not on the floor next to the dog bed!

The building's condition including cleanliness, layout, lighting, ventilation etc. They will be looking out for things like paint cracking off the walls which could work its way into someone's wedding cake, any leaky pipes which could cause a hazard to both safety and hygiene. Making sure the kitchen is well ventilated, so you're not making cupcakes in a candle lit, dusty cupboard. That kind of thing.

How you manage what you do to make sure food is safe and so they can be confident those standards will be maintained in future. This one is all about systems and processes: having things like a cleaning schedule, labels, sealable containers etc.

It is essential that these elements are met to ensure the food served or sold is safe to eat. Luckily, most of this comes down to common sense but for added reassurance, if you're in the UK you can download what's called the '**Safer Food, Better Business**' pack which has a lot of information on your kitchen and what you should know.

You can get this from the Food Standards Agency website for free. I printed mine out and put it in a ring binder so I could always check it when needed. Some of the information in it, such as meat temperatures, will not apply to you but you need to read it and fill out **all** the relevant information, including cleaning schedules and your details etc. *You can lose a rating point just for not having your paperwork filled in.*

I remember when I had my kitchen inspected. I was terrified. I kept a clean and tidy kitchen anyway but I can remember the night before and the morning of the inspection, cleaning even the cleanest of sinks, just to be sure. I had organised all my cupboards and fridge shelves. I had all my paperwork ready for inspection. So, imagine my disappointment when the officer didn't look in every single one of my cupboards. I felt like running around the kitchen opening doors at random saying "LOOK! So clean! So organised!".

I want to take a minute to brag however, and say that my little red country kitchen got five stars, too. I was very pleased with that, considering what it originally looked like!

The ratings are as follows;

⚫ Very Good

⚫ Good

⚫ Generally Satisfactory

⚫ Improvement Necessary

⚫ Major Improvement Necessary

⚫ Urgent Improvement Necessary

You are then rated at the time of inspection and you're given a fancy window sticker with your rating to display in your kitchen. If the top rating of '5 - *Very Good*' is not given, the officer will explain to you what improvements need to be made and what action you can take to improve your hygiene rating. You can legally trade at any rating, even 0. But you will need to follow the guidelines given to you.

Once this is in your mind, you'll find yourself noticing these green and black signs everywhere you go. "Ooh, the pub we go to is a 5!", "Errm.. the place down the road is only a 3!". "OMG, did you see that place? It's a 0!". Just a sample of the car conversations you may have in the coming weeks. It's certainly what I started doing anyway!

Your ratings are not just for you or to be on display, they are also made public so anyone can search for them on the Food Standards Agency website.

If you get a rating you're not happy with, you have two options, you have the right to make an appeal in writing and you can do this through the Food Standards Agency website or, you can re-quest a re-visit from your local authority once the changes and advice given to you at the time of inspection have been put into place.

It's not as scary as it sounds - I had a very nice lady for mine who had a look around my kitchen and equipment, asked me a few questions about orders, and checked up on my paperwork to make sure that I was following the right processes ensuring the safety to anyone who ordered from me. She also asked to see my filled out '*Safer Food, Better Business*' pack, so *make sure you download it*, have a good read through and fill in all the necessary sections.

Remember, the people that come and check are human too and you can talk to them, both before they come and while they are there. Ask them any questions you may have and they'll be happy to help. They aren't there to catch you out, they want you to get the highest rating just as much as you do. Try not to stress about it like I did!

There are certain things to be aware of in your kitchen when it comes to your inspection. I have done a lot of research over the years and this information not only varies from council to council but even down to which officer you get on the day, but I thought it best to advise you of these things that I found to be true when I set up my business.

Sinks. At least one sink must be provided for washing purposes, ideally two, but this isn't always possible in a home kitchen. Even if you have a dishwasher that will be taking care of your mixing bowls. It is important you have appropriate *hand washing* facilities including hot and cold water, soap and hygienic hand drying capabilities such as disposable paper towels. I know some people in the past have been fine with a double sink (with the smaller being used as a hand wash basin when working) and some with a washing up bowl, which is why I advise speaking to your local authority if you're worried. I didn't have a double sink or any other means so I had a separate hand wash basin installed in the corner of my kitchen just to be sure, although as I say, seek advice from your local authority before commencing any building work.

Pets. I've seen several comments and concerns about this one, but having pets and running a cake business from home is fine. However, you must consider how you will prevent any contamination (animal hair etc.) from getting into your kitchen and the cakes. The obvious one is to make sure you have a kitchen door that can shut properly and that pets are not allowed in the kitchen when you are working.

If you've got kitties that like to explore up on sides, you just need to make sure all surfaces or equipment they could be in contact with are thoroughly cleaned and sanitised prior to you starting any baking. This does sound like common sense, I know, but it's best to inform the officer who comes to inspect your premises that you have already thought about your furry friends!

Temperatures. One thing that was checked thoroughly in my kitchen was the temperature of my fridge. It is advised that fridge temperatures are to be set to 5°C to keep food safe from the spread of bacteria and your fridge should be running at a temperature of 8°C or below. However, the numbers on the dial in the fridge are not usually an indication of temperature. It is recommended that you purchase a *fridge thermometer*. They are cheap and easy to get hold of, I got mine from eBay.

Nuts! To avoid any cross contamination, I always keep nuts, and ingredients that have nuts in, such as *marzipan*, in a separate, sealed box. Whilst, if you're working from home you cannot say you are working out of a nut-free kitchen, (unless you don't have anything with nuts in at all. Same goes for gluten free), you still need to do your best to put them away safely so they don't contaminate other ingredients. I will be going into more detail about allergens below.

Storage. Where are you putting everything? Where do you store your ingredients? A little more care and attention needs to be paid to your baking ingredients because this is something that will be checked. It needs to be somewhere clean and dry, off the floor and able to be shut away. So, for example keeping bags of flour on the floor is not ok, but keeping them in a low cupboard with a door that shuts properly is fine. You must treat it with a little more respect than your everyday items.

First Aid Kit. Hopefully you'll never need one, but I'm sure by now we've all had a kitchen accident, haven't we? (I'm not allowed near a cheese grater anymore because I have had too many accidents). You will need a **Catering First Aid Kit** in an accessible location but not in the way. I kept mine up on a shelf above my desk in the kitchen. The difference between a catering first aid kit and a normal one is that it will come with blue plasters as standard. This is to allow visibility should the plaster come off in any way.

Labelling ingredients. Unlike when we use half a tin of beans and chuck the other half with the lid pushed back on in the fridge to use another day, we should be warier with baking ingredients. Make sure anything you have opened out of its original packaging is clearly labelled with a use-by date. You can buy handy stickers for this online. Mine came in a big roll.

Washing machines. A common concern of those wanting to run a cake business from home is the varying advice available online about washing machines. Some forums I have read have advised people to get the washing machine out of the kitchen, which is fine if you have a laundry room available to you, but washing machines are generally found in domestic kitchens. Having looked at advice from several councils around the UK, this is usually fine but something you need to consider: *you need to ensure no washing is undertaken at the same time as you are baking for your business.*

Edible Glitter. If you've been baking and cake decorating for a little while now, you may have seen 'edible glitter' being sold in shops and at trade shows. Tiny holographic sprinkles sure to add sparkle to your creations.

I used to love the stuff and would use it in abundance. Then in 2014 things changed when a company was successfully prosecuted by trading standards for breaching food safety legislation by selling cake glitter which was not of the nature demanded and for supplying a non-approved food additive.

It all got a little messy. Since then, any glitter labelled as '*non-toxic*' is only permitted for contact with food if it is applied to *removable non-food inedible items*, such as artificial flowers and figures etc. which are placed on food for decoration, provided they meet the requirements of food contact materials legislation (European Regulation 1935/2004). They should include instructions which have an indication that they should not be consumed. The glitter on these products should be fixed so it does not fall onto the cake, and it should be clear that the non-food items decorated with glitter should be removed entirely from the cake before consumption.

You now **must** look out for wording on the label specifically stating '*edible*'. You can find more information about edible glitter on the Food Standards Agency website.

Food Safety & Hygiene

While you are waiting for your local authority to come and inspect your kitchen (depending on how busy they are, this usually takes a few weeks, or at least, it did with me in both kitchens I have worked from), you need to get your **NVQ Level 2 - Food Safety and Hygiene (Catering)**. The food safety officer will ask to see this certification when they visit and some insurance companies may ask to see this too.

There are lots of courses available at colleges and cake schools. It should be relatively easy to find one near you with a quick internet search. However, if like me you prefer to do it at home in your own time, I used the **Virtual College** *Level 2 Food Safety & Hygiene for Catering (including City & Guilds Accredited Certificate)*. It cost me £15 + VAT to take this course and download your certificate or £25 + VAT to have your certificate sent to you (Prices correct as of Aug 2017). I opted for this one purely because I wanted the fancy silver seal on my certificate, but it's up to you, which option to take.

As with the 'Safer Food, Better Business' pack there will be elements of the NVQ that aren't really applicable to your business.

There is only one catering qualification unfortunately and it's a 'one size fits all' approach but it is all worth knowing, especially if you're working out of your kitchen. It covers food law, food illnesses, food safety hazards and contamination, food preservation and Hazards Analysis and Critical Control Points (HACCP).

The online course took me about 2-3 hours to complete, but if you would rather do it over a few days, it records your progress so you don't have to go back to the start each time.

At the end of the course, there is a test which consists of 30 multiple choice questions. You are required to achieve a 75% pass mark. Further attempts may be given by contacting the online support team.

Once you have your certificate there is no set time for how long it is valid, however it is generally industry recognised that food hygiene certificates are renewed every three years.

Allergens

It's handy to know that as of December 2014, the laws around allergens changed. As a baker, you are likely to come in contact with several ingredients that can cause serious harm to those with allergies. It is now the responsibility of the baker, to clearly mark and label any goods for sale that contain those allergens.

There are 14 major allergens which need to be mentioned when they are used as ingredients:

Cereals containing gluten; Crustaceans; Eggs; Fish; Peanuts; Nuts; Celery; Mustard; Soybeans; Milk; Molluscs; Sesame Seeds; Sulphur dioxide and sulphites; Lupin.

As a baker, you shouldn't need to worry too much about some of these (crustacean cake, anyone?) but you will need to be aware of them all, and how to label your products accordingly.

The easiest and most effective way of doing this, I've found, is with Allergen Stickers. Lots of companies are doing these now and are easy to find with a quick internet search.

When this first came about, the stickers were just a small check box, now you can get lovely looking personalised ones with your business name on them, designed according to your logo and in all sorts of pretty colours. Whenever you make a cake, you just tick off the allergens from the list that are in the cake (most likely eggs, nuts and possibly milk) and then stick this to the front of the box.

When the cake is collected or delivered you need to direct the client's attention to the sticker so they are aware. It is also something that should be taken into consideration when you take a cake order.

It's all well and good someone wanting a delicious chocolate cake with chocolate frosting but if you've used a popular chocolate hazelnut spread and then find out the birthday boy is allergic to nuts, you'll find yourself making a replacement cake at three in the morning the day before the party! *I may or may not be talking from experience there…*

You must ensure that customers have access to full ingredient information for products. You can read more about allergens on the Food Standards Agency website.

I know it sounds like I'm going on about these things but there are people who have serious allergies and you don't want to be responsible for making anyone sick.

Tools & Ingredients

Whenever you start a new business venture, there will always be set up costs. Now, depending on how big your cake decorating obsession has become before you decided to turn it into a career, you may already have quite a few of the tools I've listed below. I highly recommend investing a bit of money into good quality equipment for your business that will not only be beneficial to a great end-result, but will now also be a business expense and therefore tax deductible - win!

Here are my top 10 tools for cake decorating which have helped me so much:

1. *A large (16 inch) non-stick rolling pin.* My favourite ones are the white polyethylene ones which have a polished non-stick surface. I much prefer these to the traditional wooden ones as they won't leave any marks on your icing and they are much easier to keep clean. They come in varying sizes for all different kinds of project. I recommend a super big one for icing cakes.

2. *Marzipan/icing spacers*. These are invaluable to me. I use them with every cake I make. They are little strips of plastic that sit either side of the icing you roll out to ensure an even thickness.

3. *A large (10 inch) serrated cake knife*. Super sharp and professionally made, these cut through cakes like warm butter making it easy to level the top of your cakes, or as I like to call it, cutting off the top bit to taste with a cup of tea.

4. *A large (10 inch) stainless steel palette knife*. Great for spreading buttercream or ganache onto large surfaces and it also makes lifting and moving cakes very easy indeed.

5. *A cake leveller*. I can't cut through the middle of a cake in a straight line with a knife to save my life, so a cake leveller is perfect for splitting your sponges evenly. They are usually very reasonably priced and come in a variety of sizes. I recommend buying a big one though which will cater for all sizes of cake.

6. *A small, cranked palette knife*. I use this one to spread buttercream on the inside layers of a cake as well as for crumb coating. With the cranked shaped handle, it works with the tilt of your wrist to make decorating so much easier, giving you a nice smooth finish.

7. *A scribe*. This little tool is basically a long, thin metal point on a handle. It's perfect for marking out spaces on your cake, lines, where decorations will be placed and my favourite use, bursting any unwanted air bubbles in your icing.

8. *A wide paintbrush.* I recommend buying a food grade one, specifically from a cake shop as these will be made so that the little bristles don't come off and make their way into your cake. You can use this for fixing on decorations with edible glue and use it when dry, to brush off any excess icing sugar, cornflour or bits of icing from your cake or decorations.

9. *Edible glue.* Store bought or home-made, it's the best for sticking decorations onto your cake (I don't advise using water as this can dissolve your hard work!). It's also good for sticking icing to your cake boards, because naked boards should be out-lawed (in my opinion).

10. *Side scraper.* A metal or a plastic one, both are good. These look like something you would see in a plasterer's tool bag, but they are brilliant for going around your cake to smooth your buttercream, providing a great finish when crumb coating your cakes.

Outside of my top ten, I recommend a few other purchases too as follows:

Tins

Now you're a professional baker, you will need more than your standard 22cm Victoria sponge, loose-bottom cake tin found in most household cupboards. There's nothing wrong with these tins at all, and I've made many a tasty cake in them but I would recommend getting yourself a few different sizes to cover all bases. That way you're ready for whatever order a customer throws your way! The tins I use and the ones I've had the most success with over the years, are seamless anodised aluminium with straight sides and a secure base. They come in sizes from a tiny 3" all the way up to monster 16" in round, square, oblong, heart, oval and more. They are definitely an investment but if you buy good quality tins, they will last you years. I've used mine hundreds and hundreds of times and they still look as good and as strong as the day I bought them.

Stand Mixer

In the first 6 months of my business, I went through 4 hand mixers. FOUR! They kept breaking and wearing out as they simply weren't up to the abuse I was giving them. They are fine if you're making a cake once in a blue moon, but for the amount of baking I was doing every week, I needed something a little more hard-wearing in the form of a stand mixer. There are some great ones on the market right now. I did a little re-search on my social media channels as I wanted to know what mixers my readers were using in their kitchens, so I asked two questions;

1) What mixer do you have?

2) What mixer do you want? (If different from the one you have!) and why?

The results were pretty conclusive with two of the big names leading the way; *KitchenAid* and *Kenwood*. The KitchenAid won the majority with the Kenwood Chef coming second. Some people shared pictures of Kenwood mixers that had been handed down to them and still worked as strongly today as the day it came out of the box! Now THAT is a well-made product.

There is no denying the KitchenAid is a leader in its field but being one of the most expensive mixers on the market, does it live up to the hype? According to my Facebook readers, it really does. With most who have one, saying how much they love it and would never change it and a further 10% of those who answered claiming ownership of a rival make, stating that if money were no object, a KitchenAid would be sitting on the side instead.

There are a lot of different types of mixers with all sorts of attachments and add-on's available. I highly recommend doing a little research as these beauties aren't cheap, but remember, this is an investment into your business (so keep the receipt!). Have a look around, read some reviews, both industry and independent and make a choice based on your business needs (and your kitchen colour!).

Ingredients

When you're baking one or two cakes a month, a quick trip down to your local supermarket may be all that you need, however depending on how many cakes you're making in a month, it may be worth getting a wholesalers account (such as Costco, Makro, Bookers etc.) and taking a monthly trip to buy your ingredients in bulk. It will certainly save you money in the long run. It's fine to pop to the supermarket if you're short of something but I found buying all my ingredients from supermarkets 500g or 1 kilo at a time was really eating into my profit margin.

I would go up to the wholesalers every few months and buy massive bags of flour and sugar, big bottles of vanilla essence and anything else I needed (I would always bring home a big tray of sushi too. Not for the cakes, I just really like sushi. Especially in bulk). I would then store these ingredients in big tubs I had bought with giant matching scoops (think an oversized, bakers themed pick n mix). You may not need the bulk items, especially when you're starting out and you're not making too many cakes a week, but it's worth a shopping trip to see how much money you could save by doing it this way.

You will, of course, find ingredients that you like and ones you don't.

You'll grow to have preferences if you don't already and that's completely fine. I am a firm believer in you using whatever works best for you. However, I do recommend using good quality ingredients wherever possible.

I wrote an article about two different Victoria sponge cakes I made. One with 'premium' ingredients and one with 'budget' ingredients. To my surprise, it was quite a divisive article. I wrote it and made the cakes from a purely inquisitive point of view, I wasn't telling people one was better than the other at all. What I will say, however, was the cake made with the premium ingredients had a better rise, a better bake and tasted a lot better (according to my panel of independent cake testers, so not just based on my opinion).

This result did surprise me as I hadn't expected there to be too much difference between the two.

I thought most 'premium' products were all talk. I documented my findings and I was met with a lot of comments which sounded like 'well I've been using supermarket budget brand for years and haven't had any complaints,' ranging through to 'I only use premium ingredients in my cakes. Have done for years and haven't had any complaints.' You get the idea.

You can use the cheapest, the most expensive or a nice middle ground. How you run your business and what you use to bake with is entirely up to you and whatever gets you the best results.

Self-Employment

When starting a business, you must make sure you tell HMRC that you are now self-employed so that they know you need to use the Self-Assessment system to pay tax. You need to do this even if you're going to be running your cake business part-time, if you have a second job or if you are in receipt of any benefits.

Even if in the first few months of starting your career as a cake decorator you only bake 2 commission cakes and make a grand total of £12.76 profit, you **must** declare your income and pay any relevant tax. It's quick and easy to do. Head over to the HMRC website to register your new business. The easiest way to start a business in the UK is to become a '*sole trader*'. This means that only you own the business and you can work alone or employ other people. It may be different outside of the UK but the information should be relatively easy to find online where you are.

CAKES BAKES & BUSINESS

To become a sole trader in the UK you must:

✓ Have a National Insurance number

✓ Register for self-assessment with HM Revenue and Customs (HMRC)

✓ Trade under your own name or choose a business name

You have until the 31st January following the end of the tax year in which you started trading to register but I recommend doing it straight away so you have your reference numbers and you can keep on top of it all.

If you fail to register as self-employed within the deadline you can be liable for a penalty charge. The penalty charge can be reduced to nil if you let them know within the next 12 months after the penalty period has started. So really, they are giving you a LOT of time to tell them but it is all backdated to when you first started trading.

A penalty charge depends on the amount of tax you should pay and whether it was a deliberate non-declaration or not. You will be charged a percentage of the tax due to date, up to 100%, with the minimum penalty being £300. *So, get it done, get registered.*

I cannot stress just how important this step is in setting up your business. If you don't register to be self-employed but continue to work and take money and get caught doing so, on top of a penalty charge, you can be prosecuted for tax evasion.

If, after all these warnings about penalties and potential prosecutions, you still think 'well, I'm not going to be making a lot, I just won't declare, they will never know, will they?' I will tell you now, chances of you getting caught are at an all-time high. Your information being given in to HMRC by someone else is still one of the biggest ways they can catch you out. However, there is also a computer system being used that looks at algorithms and personal information so it's becoming easier for them to see who is trying to cheat the system. They also employ mystery shoppers, people who check on Facebook and Google for new businesses to make sure they are registered. Tax evasion is really hot, now and it's much easier for HMRC to go after Jo Bloggs Bakery than it is for them to target a large, international, possibly tax evading company.

Once registered, I recommend getting yourself an accountant who will file your tax return before January 31st each year for your income up to 5 April the previous year. Having an account-ant may seem costly when you are starting out, but accountants will save you money in the long run. Their expertise will save you tax, avoid potential pitfalls, ensure deadlines are met, plan-ahead and act proactively with new laws and legislation, ensuring you are meeting your legal requirements.

I'm lucky enough that my accountant is a good friend of mine, Vikki from *Striped Leopard Accountancy*, and each January I don't know what I would do without her. She makes the whole process a breeze and completely stress free.

If you're in the UK, you can earn £11,500 tax free (as of 2017/18) per annum, but there will be a Class 4 National Insurance deduction due on profits over £8,164 at 9%.

As your home is becoming your new office, a percentage of your bills will be tax deductible. The best way to do this is to add up the following for the tax year (March-April); mortgage interest, (interest element only) or rental amount, water, rates, gas & electric, cleaning and broadband. Divide this by the number of rooms in your property (excluding bathrooms) and multiply it by the number of rooms used for your business and the percentage of time they are used for. The figure you get is your allowable expense.

Don't forget to 'introduce' into your business the things you use which you already own. For example, your laptop, office furniture, baking equipment. etc. Record it all as capital expenditure at today's values.

There are also lots of options available for start-up business loans, grants and other financial help. There is the New Enterprise Allowance which is obtained through the Job Centre. You may be eligible for this if you're over 18, can show your business idea is viable and you are in receipt of either Jobseekers Allowance or Income Support. With the New Enterprise Allowance, you are assigned a business mentor who will provide support and advice on becoming self-employed and setting up your business. Once you've made a business plan and you've been approved you can get a weekly allowance worth up to £1274 over 26 weeks (as of August 2017) and a loan to help with start-up costs.

There are also government-backed loans available to start or grow your business. To apply for a loan you must have, or plan to start, a UK-based business that hasn't been fully trading for more than 24 months. You also need to live in the UK and be at least 18 years old. Start Up Loans are government-backed and charge a fixed interest rate of 6% per year and are available from 1 to 5 years. There's no application fee and no early repayment fee. You'll also get free support and guidance to help write your business plan, and successful applicants can get 12 months of free mentoring.

All this information is specifically for UK residents and is correct as of August 2017.

If you are in receipt of any benefits, these may also change

If you are in receipt of any benefits, these may also change when going self-employed. The best thing to do is to call the Department for Work and Pensions (DWP) and discuss with them any change of circumstances. If you don't report a change or a mistake and continue to get benefits, you might have to pay some of the money back. You might also get a £50 penalty.

With regards to keeping a note of your incomings and outgoings, there are lots of apps you can download and cloud based software you can use to help with this. An easy way to start though is to use a spreadsheet.

I'm not the best with figures (hence the need for an accountant!) but I have a spreadsheet for my incoming money and one for my outgoing.

I set the headers up like this;

MONEY OUT / 2015 - APRIL 2016

Date	Company	Amount	Payment	Referenc
1/12	Wilko	£10.55	Card	INV001
2/12	Sainsbury	£32.20	Card	INV002
2/12	Iced Jems	£25.70	Card	INV003
2/12	Poundland	£8.00	Cash	INV004

MONEY IN / 2015 - APRIL 2016

Date	Product	Amount	Payment	Receipt No
6/4	Cake C.Name	£150	BACS	21
7/4	Cupcakes J.Name	£40	Cash	22
13/4	Cake Deposit	£25	Paypal	23
17/4	Cake A.Name	£75	Cash	24

It doesn't have to be complicated. It's quite a simple system I use but it works.

Every month I go through my bank account and fill out the spreadsheet for everything to do with my business.

I keep *all* my receipts for everything I spend on the business - every pack of flour, every cake board, every sprinkle! Even if I have bought other items as well as business items in the same shopping trip, I highlight the items relevant and keep it. I write at the top of the receipt a reference number. I then enter this reference number on my spreadsheet (under receipt no.) so if my accountant ever needs to check my records, it will be very easy to find.

I also give every customer a receipt (as well as a cake order form, we will talk about these later). That way there is proof of the transaction of money on both sides. You can pick up a cheap carbon copy receipt book from most stationary shops or spend a bit on a custom-made receipt pad. Either does the job just fine!

If I had a BACS or PayPal payment sent through to my bank account, I would send an email receipt which was just a document I made on my laptop with their contact information, cake information, monies paid and monies owing. Make sure to have a copy of everything you do in writing to cover yourself always.

Nothing said in this chapter is meant to spook you. I know it sounds serious but I promise it's all very doable and everything I have gone through with regards to penalties and charges are all worst-case scenario, but I want you to go into this being aware. The last thing I would want you to do, is get in trouble!

Insurance

You wouldn't buy a car without getting it insured, you probably buy holiday insurance and I'm guessing your home is insured too. Similarly, you must buy insurance for your new cake business.

The council will sometimes ask to see your insurance paperwork when checking your kitchen (mine did) and if you are planning on having a stand at a craft fair or farmers market, (I talk about the benefits of these in the Marketing chapter!), then you should be aware that most of them are now asking to see insurance certificates for you to trade there, because if anything happens and you're not covered, it falls to them as the event hosts.

I know we don't set out each day for something bad to happen but the reality is, sometimes it does. Should the worst happen, you know you'll be covered for all eventualities.

Common types of cake related insurance claims include; An unexpected outbreak of food poisoning is deemed to have come from your cake affecting several members of the public, delivering a wedding cake to a venue you accidentally knock an expensive table ornament over which smashes, and a foreign object falls into your cake or icing mixture and a customer bites into it causing them injury.

If a client suffers an allergic reaction or gets ill from one of your cakes, or if they have an accident when collecting their order, then you could face legal consequences and a substantial financial penalty if you're not correctly insured. I know these instances may seem very unlikely, but for the small price of monthly insurance it's worth it for the peace of mind.

Insurance isn't just to cover your customers either, it's also to cover you. Most cake business insurance providers will have packages and policies that will also cover and replace your tools and equipment, if they are stolen or damaged for example. Some even have a personal accident benefit which offers a *'Capital sum in relation to death, loss of limbs or eyes or resulting in permanent total disablement whilst performing your Sugar-craft activities, including collection and delivery.'* which sounds, frankly terrifying but hey, at least you'll be covered!

I used to get my insurance from the British SugarCraft Guild. You must become a member of the BSG to purchase insurance. Membership is £24 for the year and for that you get access to the BSG meetings, (plus a small charge that goes towards the venue each meeting), where you can watch sugar-craft demon-strations as well as receiving the British SugarCraft Newsletter as published.

There are three different types of insurance packages you can buy from BSG;

Public & Products Liability Only. Starting at £20.50 per year.

Public & Products plus all risks cake cover. Starting at £75.50 per year.

Public & Products plus all risks cake cover and money cover. Starting at £86.50 per year.

(All prices are correct, at time of publication 2017).

For a starting cover of £2 million, it's very reasonably priced. However, please be advised this insurance is only for those whose turnover from their Sugar-craft activities does not exceed £8,500.00 per annum. If you are making more than this, you will need to find a different insurance company, however it really is a great place to start with. Have a look at their website, read through the insurance policy completely and see which plan would be best for you.

It really depends on how much cover you think you'll need for your business. If in doubt, start small and work your way up.

Since *the Great British Bake Off* came to our screens in 2010, it has steadily grown in popularity year upon year. Some would say bringing baking into our homes on prime-time TV is partly responsible for the rise in home baking businesses.

Owing to this new-found popularity, lots of other large insurance companies are now offering insurance packages specifically made for cake decorators from home. It's worth sitting down one afternoon with a cuppa and having a look around online to find the best deal for you. A quick 'insurance for cake business' search provided me with tons of results, more choice than I had a few years ago which tells me it's certainly on the rise (baking pun). It doesn't matter where you get insurance from, just please make sure you get it.

You will also need to consider that if customers will be collecting cakes from your home, you will need to speak to your home insurance provider. You need to make sure you are covered in case a customer hurts themselves on your property. In my old flat (which was on the first floor and that itself came with its own health and safety concerns!) there was a hidden step as you walked in the front door which I myself tripped over countless times. If I knew a customer was due to collect a cake I would always open the door, shake their hand and exclaim 'mind the step!'.

The last thing you want is for a customer to trip over on the way in or worse, trip on the way out, taking the cake with them, smashing your hard work into a thousand pieces as they head for the floor and potentially injure themselves with you being liable. Again, sounds unlikely, but you need to be aware of these things. Your monthly home insurance may go up slightly but as I say, it will be worth it in the long run should the worst happen.

Something else to consider, is that if you are planning on delivering cakes, you must speak with your car insurance provider for the same reason. You may be covered by your current plan, especially if you are only delivering the odd cake here and there. But give them a call and ask them, as you may need extra cover if you are using the car for business purposes. (However, if you go with the BSG 'all-risks' cover, it will cover loss or damage to the cake whilst at home, at a venue or in transit. So, it is worth reading the fine print). If in doubt, speak to your current insurance providers. They will be able to offer the best advice to make sure you are covered for every eventuality.

Marketing

So, your kitchen is signed off. You've registered to be self-employed and you're insured. Let me be one of the first to say congratulations on your new business! Now for the most important part - getting customers!

There are so many ways you can market yourself to tell people about your new cake business. I'm going to take you through a few of my favourite ways below which worked well for me.

Firstly however, something fun to sit down and think about if you haven't already, is your business name! You can use your own name "Britt's Bakery", "Ciara's Cakes", "Jodie's Cakes & Bakes" for example or come up with something entirely different. You can make it personal if you like, to make it special. I know of someone who set up a business name in memory of her nan, which I thought was so thoughtful.

My original thought for my own business name was The Fondant

Fairy. I liked the way it sounded and I had some pretty cool ideas for logos. But after a short time, I fell out of love with it for a few reasons; one was that 'fondant' is a very American term and being in the UK I didn't want to cause any confusion as to what it was I did. Also, I had realised I wasn't always working with fondant. I knew if I didn't completely love my business name, it probably wasn't the one for me. So, I soon abandoned that one.

I have always been a blogger. Writing has been one of my passions since I was at school and journaling is a hobby of mine.

My blog, before I started baking, was called '*She Who Dares*', taken from the phrase 'fortune sides with she who dares'. It only took a 10-minute chat and a cuppa with my friend Ali to work out *She Who Bakes* would be a nice, easy transition!

That was back in 2010 and I still love the name today. It's best to choose something that's not likely to change, as it's what people will get to know you as. I've had people come up to me at business networking meetings saying, "You're *She Who Bakes* aren't you?" even though I've got a name badge on saying 'Britt'. So, it's got to be something you don't mind people calling you (although in the end people may just call you the cake lady or cake guy).

It's worth checking online to make sure the name you have in mind isn't already in use by someone local, which could cause confusion. It's best to check an internet search engine, like Google as well as social media.

Some businesses may have a Facebook page but not a website.

If you've got your heart set on a name and there is someone already using it but they are half a world away, I would say you're probably alright. But if they are only 5 miles down the road, I would advise picking something else.

If you're only planning on making cupcakes for customers, something like 'Kate's Cupcakes' would work really well. However, be advised if you're planning on moving into doing bigger cakes and wedding cakes etc., you may lose out on enquiries as the public may assume you only do cupcakes, and may not even contact you about it.

If you're really struggling for a name idea, there are plenty of lists available online which may provide you with a slice of inspiration (see what I did there? Love a pun).

Once you've got your business name sorted, it's worth investing in a great logo to help you stand out and establish your brand. If you're talented with a bit of photoshop, you can create something really personal. However, if like me you aren't that way inclined, you can get a logo custom made.

I knew roughly what I wanted with mine, swirly writing, pink background and a little cartoon version of me, because why not.

I found a lovely company called *Purple Scrunch* who were recommended to me by a friend. Laura, who owns the business and is very talented, was super helpful with my logo design. She created something based on my vision and after one minor tweak it was perfect. I love it and still use it today, even if I don't have bright red hair anymore! Once you've got your logo, you can then use it on all sorts of fun branding! Laura, for example, provides so many stationery options including allergen stickers (which I mentioned above in the *Your Kitchen* chapter), Wedding Cake Consultation Forms, Terms & Conditions and Disclaimers and Cake Order forms (which I will discuss later).

You may find that once you have a logo you love, you'll be putting it on everything! I remember buying notebooks and magnets and even a mug with my new logo on before I'd even taken one customer order, it was all so exciting and you are totally allowed to be excited and have fun with it.

Here are a few tools I used for marketing my new business in the early days and still use today:

Word Of Mouth

When the time comes, where you've had your kitchen looked at and you've registered to be self-employed, unless you've been keeping your hobby and career aspirations a closely guarded secret, your friends and family will all probably know you make cakes. You may have even consulted with them before taking the plunge to the entrepreneur life. You can usually fill up the first few weeks, if not months of your order books by word of mouth from your biggest cheerleaders.

Never underestimate how many people your loved ones know that you don't. Tell your nearest and dearest you're now open and taking orders and advise them to give out your contact information.

The more cakes you make, the more people will know about you.

I remember on one occasion I made a cake for a child's birthday party and that in turn brought me seven new orders for the coming months from parents who attended the party for their own children. Do a good job and people will talk about you, recommendation is so powerful; I know businesses that have existed for years on word of mouth alone to get clients.

Website

I personally believe that all businesses need a good website. For the first year of my business, I solely used my blog. This was fine for a while and certainly gave me something I could show to people to prove I was real. I even bought the domain name through a third party and directed all searches to my blog. This, however, wasn't without it's pitfalls. When you host your website on an external source like my original blog was, you are limited in what you can and cannot do.

For example, I couldn't have separate pages to show a gallery, information, contact form etc. I couldn't categorise anything, it was just one long scroll of content. Then about a year into managing it, I had a massive problem. Overnight, I had lost everything. Every post, every picture, everything.

Someone had reported my page for *'inappropriate content'*. I can assure you, while my cakes may look especially naughty, that was the only content on the site. I hadn't broken any rules at all but unfortunately, a big site like the one I hosted my original blog on should cover its back and work on a 'deactivate now - ask questions later' attitude.

I was, understandably, devastated. Luckily, I knew someone who was more clued up on this kind of thing than I am. He managed to salvage about 75% of my pictures, blog posts and recipes. It was that day I called and spoke to a web company about having a 'proper website'.

I had a meeting with Neil and Carrie who run *Clockwork Moggy*, a web design company recommended to me by a friend.

I sat down with them and told them what it was I wanted my website to do, what the purpose of it was and what I wanted it to look like. They took all of that into consideration and designed me the website I have today.

It works really well for me and is exactly what I had envisaged. The good thing about working with a web design team is that as your business expands and evolves they can help you make the necessary changes. For example, by the time I had spoken with them about having a website, my blog was used for three main things; the blog itself, including reviews and personal posts, recipes which I had developed in my kitchen and as a gallery for customer cakes. I wanted all three of these elements to be represented clearly on my new website as well as an information/about me page and a contact me page for clients to easily send in queries.

I found my bookings went up just by having an online presence and a few months in, a large portion of my cake bookings were coming through via my website. A little while into having my new page, I had started offering cake decorating courses both in my studio in Kent and online versions and needed this information on the website as well as a little shop too. This was easily done thanks to having professionals on hand to help.

This company now host and manage my website and I have an online page I am very proud of. Be aware a bespoke website isn't cheap and should be an investment. Your domain name will cost about £10-20 a year (plus VAT). Simple web design work costing somewhere between £400-£600 and then ongoing maintenance costs of £10-£70 per month.

If you haven't got the budget and are willing and able to put the work in yourself, there are lots of free hosting sites that will fit the bill, but always make sure to back up your content and if you're using a third-party hosting site, be aware of their terms and conditions. You can buy a domain name relatively easy with a quick Google and some websites, have pre-programmed themes for your site which can be a great place to start.

Be aware however, if your website & business looks like you haven't spent any money on it, it's like putting a Tesco's value label on your product. What that means is customers will expect you to be a cheap company, they may want to haggle with you over prices and you'll have to compete with bigger companies who can mass produce products very cheaply but without the love and attention that you would put into it.

Blog

Having a blog can be an excellent marketing tool. As I've said I've been blogging for years now and could go on for days about the benefits of it, both for me personally, and professionally. But it really depends what you would use it for.

If, like me, you want to document your baking journey for people to read, as well as have tips and tutorials and reviews, then I 100% think you should be writing a blog. However, if you're reading this thinking 'Britt, I barely have the time, I just want to make cakes for people', then I would say to skip this one.

Having a blog on your website can really boost SEO (search engine optimisation) and is a great way to send traffic to your page which (if designed correctly) should ultimately end up in cake bookings. But if you're not going to use it then there is little point in having one. A blog is something that needs regular upkeep (think a modern day tamagotchi) and if left alone or not given regular attention it will die. Ok, not die, that's a bit extreme but it will be as useful to you as if you didn't blog at all. It all depends if you like the idea of blogging as I believe it should come from a place of want rather than being forced to.

But if taking photos of your work 'in progress' and talking about what you do and reviewing products and maybe even coming up with recipes, sounds like something you would be interested in then get in there and blog!

Set aside some time weekly to document your goings on. You could even do mini tutorials based on what cakes you were doing that week, which is what I did.

My little blog, which grew into an award-winning business was something that saved me, in so many ways. Picking up the Kent Digital Award for Best Blog in 2015 and being awarded 'Highly Commended' at the UK Blog Awards in 2017 were two of my best moments. I will always have a soft spot for blogging and will recommend it to everyone who will listen!

Social Marketing

Facebook

With more than a billion active users, Facebook, and social media in general, has changed the way we do business. It can be an incredibly effective way of marketing yourself. Firstly, if you're going to be using Facebook as a way of advertising what you do, make sure you are creating a business page that people can *'like'* and *'follow'* and not a personal profile where people can *'add as friend'*.

A little while ago Facebook cracked down on people using personal profiles as business pages. Someone I know had theirs deleted completely meaning she lost all her posts, pictures and connections. If, like me, you've been using Facebook for years and you have lots of personal stuff on there you don't want to lose including holiday snaps and family memories, I would recommend not taking the risk. You can of course mention to your Facebook friends you will be starting a business, but then share your business page instead.

Setting up a business page doesn't cost anything, only takes a few minutes and you can invite all your family and friends to *'like'* it and *'share'* it with their contacts. As I've said, never underestimate how many people your loved ones know.

A Facebook business page is a great way of displaying your work for people locally. You can upload photo albums as well as an engaging profile and cover photo. Pages also allow for reviews which lets potential customers know of your high standard and they will be able to see previous customers praising your work.

In the early days when you are starting out and you haven't had any commissions, ask your friends and family to write reviews to start you off. They will know what your cakes are like and will (hopefully) be some of the best people to say good things about you.

Another benefit of Facebook, are the *free groups* you can join. They act as a forum. If you find and join buying and selling groups such as 'Facebay' in your area as well as 'Wedding Swap Shops', you can upload pictures of your work with a little description of who you are and what areas you cover and how people can get in contact to buy from you. This is free advertising and was an essential tool for me when I was looking for work.

A big tip though, is to try and not be offended when you post a beautiful cake picture of your hard work for someone to simply write 'how much?' on it. They know not what they do. They don't know that each cake is custom designed and bespoke made. That just pricing the cake up for an occasion, considering how many it will serve and what ingredients it needs, takes time and effort. They are just treating it as a shop window.

In this instance, I would usually reply to them privately with a bit of information on my prices and what I can offer, and then on their public comment I would add 'I have sent you a message'. Just so they and other people know you haven't ignored the enquiry, but you've dealt with it privately.

One piece of advice I have though, with regards to these buying and selling groups, is to *not* get yourself caught up in a 'race to the bottom' price war. There are so many people making cakes nowadays but I believe there is room for everyone. However, one day when I was browsing buy and sell groups, (I buy a lot of second hand furniture and upcycle with chalk paint, another hobby of mine!), I saw someone had posted a picture of a cake they had found online with a question 'I want this cake for next weekend. Can people give me quotes please?'.

Seems harmless enough, right?

What ensued in the comment section was nothing short of a free for all.

A cake maker had commented that she could do it for an amount, let's say £60. Then a minute later another cake maker said she could do it for £55. Then another for £50. They were

CAKES BAKES & BUSINESS

all undercutting one another publicly to get the sale. Then after it had halved in value to around £30, insults started being thrown around and before you know it, it had got quite nasty and very personal. Completely unnecessary.

Whenever I saw any of these posts and I was looking for cake work, I would reply to the person who asked the original question with a few pictures of similar cakes I'd made if I had any, as well as my prices and a way to contact me. I would then leave it well alone. If they got back to me and booked in, great! If they got back to me and asked to haggle I would politely explain my prices were set. If they didn't get back to me, also fine. There will always be someone who can make something for cheaper, and there will always be potential customers that go with a competitor for one reason or another, and that's ok, you keep being you and your customers will find you.

My top tips for any Facebook page;

Photos. Make sure any pictures you take of your bakes look appealing and will entice customers to buy from you. If you've got a mixing bowl on the side or a cat in the background, it can detract from what you are trying to offer. I'm not saying these need to be professional photos, I used my mobile phone for most of my gallery, but try and set the scene a little, rather than having it on a messy worktop.

70

These days you can buy really great backdrops specifically for your cakes or, a great alternative is to use wallpaper. I had a few different wallpaper samples that I used specially for my cake pictures, (unless the owner of a popular initialled hardware store is reading this, in which case, I only ever got wallpaper samples for decorating my living room...). You would be surprised at the difference it makes.

If you have a source of natural light, use it to your advantage to show off your work. I would put my cake on a table in front of a cupboard in my lounge by the window, on top of a backdrop and then stick the backdrop with blu-tak to the cupboard (a really high-tech set up I'm sure you can imagine). Work with what you've got.

Potential customers won't be able to taste cake through their screen, (what a delicious world that would be), so they have to feast with their eyes. By ensuring your photos look good enough to eat, it will invite orders. I would also advise using an app or online software to add your logo somewhere to your picture. Too many people I know, myself included, have had cake pictures stolen from Facebook pages only to be uploaded on someone else's with them claiming it was their work.

The weirdest one I had was a New York themed cake I made for a birthday, about 2 weeks after posting a picture of it a friend of mine had alerted me to a cake page in Iran, who had posted the picture on their page claiming they 'really enjoyed making it' and to 'contact them to buy it'. I was upset that someone was passing off my hard work as theirs and after multiple messages to them asking them to take it down they finally did, but having a logo will often deter people from doing this.

That said, I have had photos with my logo on stolen and used to promote other companies before, so sadly it won't stop them completely. All you can do is send them a message saying the picture is your intellectual property and ask them to remove it. If they don't you can report it to Facebook.

Keep it friendly. We all know social media can be a great outlet for when we've had a bad day or someone has wronged us, but keep that stuff away from your business page.

Post what you like on your personal page, no one is denying you of that privilege, but your business page will sometimes be the first thing potential customers see of you, so please, remember to keep it professional.

I have a '*no negativity*' rule on my Facebook page. I will only post positive, relevant content. This makes it easy for people to see what you're about. I usually post pictures of cakes I've made and pictures of cakes that have gone 'viral', or ones that I particularly like the look of.

My Facebook page has been an integral part of my business and I put a lot of that down to my use of content. Whatever you do, don't moan about customers or bad mouth other businesses. All you will do is make your page a point of gossip for other people. You may post a rant and think by deleting it, no one will see it. But this is the internet and nothing is gone forever. Just remember, talking badly about your competitors only looks bad on you.

Negative comments. While we're on the subject of less than positive content, you may be subject to negative comments. It is usually rare (thankfully) and you can deal with these how you wish.

Depending on the type of comment I recommend a few different techniques. If it is a customer who has an issue with a specific order, I would suggest you resolve this privately, replying to their public comment letting them know you have messaged them. This way people outside can see you are dealing with it. I saw a comment which descended into a full-on argument not that long ago.

A bride and groom had ordered a wedding cake and when the kitchen cut into it on the wedding day, the bottom tier had a thin layer of mould - nightmare! From what I could gather, the couple approached the baker and told them of this but were fobbed off by the baker not taking any responsibility for the mouldy cake, saying it had been stored incorrectly after collection.

The couple then took to social media and posted several pictures of the mouldy cake on the baker's Facebook page. The baker then publicly and negatively responded to the couple getting into an argument with them. This resulted in the bride and groom's family and friends giving the page 1* reviews.

I don't know the full story or what happened behind closed doors. I'm not saying the couple were in the right, I'm not saying the baker was in the right. What I am saying is *these types of complaints* should be dealt with privately and not publicly.

However, if they are negative comments purely for the sake of it written by trolls or grown adults who really should know better and find something more constructive to do with their time, I highly recommend the '**delete and block**' approach. Do not engage with them and do not publicly argue on your page. Your Facebook page is not an open forum, it's your business and you must protect it.

If there are any genuine negative comments, criticism or feedback, replying to them fairly, politely and openly is always good as it makes you look transparent and honest. Don't be disheartened, though. **You can't please everybody.**

Be engaging. One thing to remember about all social media, it's meant to be social! If people put lovely comments on your cake pictures, make sure to take the time to reply to them.

I know it can be tricky when you are doing lots of other different things and as your pages grow over time it can be hard to keep track of, but people will always buy from people they know, like and trust first. If you build up rapport with those engaging with your page, they will be more likely to order from you in the future.

Find ways to engage with your audience, this can be in the form of an opinion, for example; "I'm thinking about adding some new cupcake flavours to my range! What are your favourites?" asked with a bright image of some of your lovely cupcakes maybe. By asking something like this, not only do you get engagement from people wanting to tell you what their favourite is, it also gives you an idea of what your customers want to see from you! Too many people think they know what their customers want, without asking them first.

Another way to increase engagement is with giveaways and competitions. You should be quite careful on how you do this on Facebook now as they have brought in lots of new rules. I would advise searching on Facebook for their giveaway rules and terms of service, and reading through them fully before participating or posting a competition, as the rules do change periodically.

For example, at the time this book goes to print, competitions where pages ask you to 'share to win' are against the Facebook 'terms of service'; *Personal Timelines and friend connections must not be used to administer promotions (e.g. "share on your Timeline to enter" or "share on your friend's Timeline to get additional entries" and "tag your friends in this post to enter" are not permitted).* But just how many of them do we see daily? Remember, just because someone else is doing it, doesn't mean it's right (metaphor for life there, bakers). Check the rules, cover yourself and then plan your giveaway. You can always use a third-party competition website.

Seasonal offers are a great way to boost both engagement and sales. One thing I noticed when it came up to Christmas, Valentine's Day, Easter etc., was that if I just waited for someone to order those kinds of themed designs from me, by the time I'd made them and posted pictures online in the hope others would buy them from me too, it was usually too late.

What I would do, is about a month before the seasonal event, get your thinking apron on and bake something special for those occasions. A cupcake bouquet for Mother's Day, a Santa cake for Christmas, Easter nest chocolate cupcakes, whatever you like! Then post them on your page in plenty of time for people to see them, want them and order from you. As a little bonus, you then get to eat or gift a pre-seasonal treat!

I could go on and on about Facebook and its benefits. I love social media in all its forms for so many different uses. But I will finish this section on Facebook with, in my opinion, one of the most important aspects. ***Regular, relevant content.*** I, along with a lot of other people I know, will always check out a business Facebook page before I buy from them. I'm checking reviews, customer posts and looking for any upcoming offers. If I log on and see their last posted picture was 6 months ago or more, a part of me would wonder if they were still in business at all! Make sure to set aside the time to keep it regular, especially when you're starting out. You never know who is looking and when.

I would also advise to keep your content relevant to what you do. It's awesome if you've found a bargain for 100 daffodil bulbs up at the garden centre, but that's maybe something for your personal page and not your cake business one.

Facebook is something you should work on. You've got to set aside the time to build a great page. But it is worth it and it's where so many bakers I know, myself included, built their business from nothing.

Twitter

Next up on social media, we have Twitter. If you enjoy talking and connecting with people, Twitter is a great way of doing that. I've found it an incredible resource for professional connections as well as meeting like-minded people, some of whom have been a lifeline over the years.

You can sign up for a free profile, use your business name and shiny new logo and get out there and talk to people, in 140 characters or less. There are a lot of benefits to using Twitter for your cake business but with over 500 million Tweets being sent each day, how do you make yours stand out?

As we have already covered above, photos are an excellent resource on social media. As busy people, we do a lot of scrolling and it takes something to catch our eye for us to pay attention, a tasty looking picture is a great way to do this.

Another way to get noticed is to include Trending Topics. These are the most popular topics being discussed on Twitter at any one time based on algorithms and are tailored to you using your location, who you follow and your interests. You can use these to your advantage to get yourself noticed by Tweeting something relevant and adding a trending hashtag. For example, when the Olympics were on TV, I had made Olympic medal cupcakes. I tweeted a picture of them with the #London2012 hashtag that was trending and had enquiries off the back of it. There are weekly trending topics such as #MondayMotivation and #ThrowbackThursday that with a little imagination, you can make relevant to cake!

You can also get involved with Twitter chats and challenges where you can chat to other bakers, exchange recipes, show off your new bakes and meet like-minded people. Trust me, friends and family, while very supportive, might not be as interested when you show them the 15th new palette knife you've bought that week, but us fellow bakers will be!

The simplest and most effective way of getting noticed on Twitter is by talking to people. Follow accounts you're interested in, follow other bakers, follow celebrities, whoever you like. Start a conversation with them. Reply to tweets. Get chatting and get involved!

Instagram

Having grown to 700 million users as of April 2017, the photo editing and sharing social network, Instagram has secured its place as one of the most popular social media platforms. It's also exceptionally good for businesses who have a visual element, such as your new cake business.

I fell in love with Instagram thanks to its flattering filters but over the years it has become an integral part of my marketing strategy. Like Twitter, you can use hashtags at the end of your post to get your photos noticed by people all over the world.

You can also use local hashtags to find business nearer to home too, for example by adding local hashtags such as #Kent, #Maidstone, #London, anyone searching that will see your cakes and it's a great way to get out to a new audience.

Whereas with Twitter you have a limit on how many characters you can use in a post, you don't have those restrictions on Instagram, (there is a limit of 30 hashtags, however), so you can post in more detail about your cakes. You can talk about the flavours, about how you made it, anything you think potential customers may find interesting. I often found on Instagram my *'behind the scenes'* photos did just as well, if not better, as my staged *'perfect'* photos.

Instagram is also a really good way of having an online portfolio of your work as your profile will be just photos so it's easy to direct potential customers to your profile. Once you've made cakes, ask customers to tag your Instagram account in their photos when they post them and you can repost these photos to your followers as another way of showing off the fabulous work you have done for other people with their testimonials.

Face To Face Networking

Time to get offline and out there into the real world! When I started my business, I attended a lot of networking meetings. These are usually an hour or so long meetings, sometimes ridiculously early in the morning, comprised of local business owners. You go along, have a nice breakfast, and then depending on how the meetings are set up there is usually *'open networking'* where you can meet and chat to people about what you do, then a chance to talk about your business to the group briefly (usually 60 seconds) followed by a presentation (more about this in a moment), a bit more open networking and then home to follow up on your new leads!

There are lots of different networking groups available. Morning, lunchtime and evening are all catered for. There are women only ones, 'after hours' ones which sometimes include a glass of fizz, ones in animal sanctuaries and many more.

If you have a look online, you will be sure to find one local to suit you quickly. Some of them are no obligation and 'pay as you go', going to as many or as few as you would like, and some of them are more structured with a yearly membership to pay. With these ones, you usually make back your membership at a networking group with business referrals in the first year.

Networking can be a fantastic tool in getting out there in your local community, spreading the word about your business and getting orders in. I mean, everyone has and knows someone who has a birthday right? The further you spread the word about your new venture, the more business you will get.

Once you are a member of a networking group, you will also be able to do presentations. I did quite a few of these when I was a member of a local networking group and I got two people up to the front with me, showed them how to pipe a cupcake, gave them a piping bag each and let them at it! It was great fun and a nice interactive way for people to see, (and taste), what you do.

What I found is that networking is also fantastic for personal development and support in a business aspect. When you surround yourself with entrepreneurs and business minded people, you will be surprised how much advice you soak up like some sort of business sponge (I'm thinking a sponge dressed in a suit with a tiny sponge briefcase…). It's also a great way of representing yourself professionally.

I remember being so nervous when I went to my first networking meeting. I had never done anything like it before and was terrified people would think I was 'too young' to be in business (I was 24 at the time and was one of the youngest in the room). But I quickly learned age is nothing to do with it.

To break any ice and relieve (my) tension I brought along a box of cupcakes and it was the best decision! People loved them (everyone loves cupcakes) and through demonstrating what I could do as soon as I met someone, I went home with three orders that day. I went the following week without any cupcakes, but with a great deal of confidence and enthusiasm and was greeted warmly.

I still go networking today, both in a social and professional capacity and I love it and I always get a lot from going, including my fiancé, Tim, whom I met at a networking Christmas do!

Photos

Always, always, always take photos of your cakes. They are a brilliant marketing tool and a really nice way to track your own progress and journey. If you don't have any good photos of cakes you've made, it will be worth its weight in gold to spend a bit of money, make up some example cakes and decorate them just for taking some shots.

People eat with their eyes first. If you can show them examples of your work, they will be more likely to buy from you as they will have the confidence that you can complete their order.

I remember when I first started, I spent weeks making and decorating cakes that I ended up giving to charity, giving to friends and eating myself. They weren't cheap to make but the pictures were worth it and secured lots more orders. It's no good just telling people you make awesome cakes, you need to prove it to them. Try and get good quality photos if you can, using a digital camera or a high resolution mobile phone camera and with a nice background.

Business Cards

Cards with your business name and contact information are a

great tool to have about your person as you never know when you are going to bump into a potential customer. I've been in a taxi before now and the driver mentioned his daughter's birthday was coming up. I asked if he had thought about a cake yet and he said no, but it was next on his list! I gave him my card and made the cake the following week. You really will be surprised who you can meet, daily, who may need your services. Business cards are an excellent tool to bring with you if you go face to face networking too.

You can always meet people and ask them to find you on Facebook but they may forget or spell your business name wrong and you will have lost that enquiry for good. Giving them a card in their hand means you have a better chance of sticking in their mind. You can get them printed in so many places now at reasonable prices. If you've got your logo made up by this point, use it on the cards. Get some made up and keep them with you in your bag wherever you go!

Local Cafés

It's always worth your time to approach local cafés and businesses as a way of generating sales. Ask the café owner who supplies their cakes and cupcakes. If you become their supplier, that's regular work for you and a way of getting your cakes to the public. If you're supplying them, ask the café to put up a poster/flyer about you and your business to raise your profile locally.

Only take on this kind of venture though if you have the time. I did this briefly in the first year of being in business and I got so busy with cake orders I had to stop. If they don't need a cake or cupcake supplier or it's not something you're looking to do right now, ask local cafés and businesses to put a flyer up anyway! Some may even let you put a display cake in the window which would be great to catch the eye of passing trade in your area. If they say no, you haven't lost anything.

Farmer's Markets/ Craft Fairs

These are a fun way of getting out there and meeting your local community as well as making a bit of money. As I've said before, people will buy from those who they know, like and trust. By investing in a stand at a local farmers market or craft fair, you can show off what you can do and meet people face to face.

The stands themselves usually aren't that expensive but you do have to consider the cost of making the cakes, cupcakes and other baked goods as well as calculating how much you want to charge and how customers will take purchases home.

You can now buy individual plastic pods for both cupcakes and slices of cake, as well as standard cupcake and cake boxes. They are a great place to start and will be worth your time and money in meeting people and giving them your information. Go armed other baked goods as well as calculating how much you want to charge and how customers will take purchases home.

You can now buy individual plastic pods for both cupcakes and slices of cake, as well as standard cupcake and cake boxes. They are a great place to start and will be worth your time and money in meeting people and giving them your information. Go armed with cards and flyers for people to take away and pop your contact information into any bags of purchases. Don't forget if you're doing these kind of markets or fairs to have a copy of your insurance certificate handy.

Cake Shows

Industry shows, while maybe not the best place to get local cake business, are a great place to meet people. I'm a firm believer that there is more than enough business in this world for us all, and that my fellow cake decorator is not my competition, but my friend. All the other cake decorators around me in my area were so helpful. I became friends with a lot of them and from borrowing a cutter, to asking for a bit of help, to having someone to refer to when you are fully booked or on holiday, so much can come from collaboration as opposed to competition.

Don't be afraid to meet other cake decorators in your area. Being self-employed and working from home can be a lonely place. It's good to have the kind of people around you that understand your baking trials and tribulations. Like I say, our friends and family mean well, but they won't understand the sheer joy you will get from a perfectly iced cake.

How Much Is A Cake?

This is a very personal topic and one of the most asked questions I see on cake forums and pages. The frustrating answer unfortunately, is one I can't tell you. No one can. It is something you must come to on your own. But I can give you some of the tips I used to help you get there. I've included a cake pricing template with this book to get you started.

I personally don't believe in the *"three times the cost of your ingredients"* rule that I know some bakers use. That may work for them and that is fine, but it didn't for me and so I did it in a slightly different way. Firstly, you need to know your costs *exactly*. Down to a single egg. This means busting out a calculator and every penny of your cake needs to be worked out. You will need to consider;

Ingredients. Contrary to popular belief, this won't be the main component for costing cakes, but it will be an important one. The way I do this, is by working out how much 100g of ALL your basic ingredients cost such as flour, butter, sugar, etc. also how much it costs per egg. It will then make it a lot easier to cost per cake. I add up how much of these I have used in my recipe and write this number down. If in doubt, there are some great apps available for your smart phone that will be able to help, they don't cost very much and they are another business expense. Also, if you use online grocery shopping, the price per 100g is usually worked out for you in the description of the item.

Overheads. As you're working from home, your overheads will include your gas, electricity, water, petrol (if delivering) rent and any other costs. This is easiest to calculate if you can work it out to an hourly rate, then you can calculate how many hours it takes to bake. Have a look at your electricity bill or call your provider, they should be able to help you with this information.

Equipment. Boards, boxes, dowels, icing, ribbon and if you need to purchase a special cutter or certain tool for a commission. These all need to be included in your costs. A wedding cake I made for a friend recently cost twice as much in equipment as it did in ingredients. If not calculated correctly, it can be a large chunk of your profit.

Your time. This is the big one. This is the one most people struggle with. If you're panicking about costing for your time, know you're not alone. All creatives and self-employed people are unsure of their price tag. Think about it this way, if you were applying for a job, what is the minimum per hour you would accept? It shouldn't be any different just because you are working for yourself in your own kitchen. When you are starting out, you will almost certainly undercharge. Both for the cake and for your time. ***But please don't fear charging what you're worth***. If you don't pay yourself a decent wage, you will struggle to run this as a business. Especially if you are counting on this venture being your main source of income.

Work out your hourly rate, then work out how long you think the cake will take you to make. Add this together along with your equipment cost, overheads and ingredients and you will get a better idea of the prices you should be charging. You may think you are asking for too much. I promise you, you're not. Once you have been making cakes a few months and you realise you cannot put your heart and soul into a project for peanuts you will realise something needs to change. **Your time, your talent and YOU are worth more than that**.

For the first few months of my business, I worked out I was being paid £1.21 per hour. I was losing money rapidly and I was contemplating getting a second job. Instead, I worked out my costings, I upped my prices respectively and guess what happened? I started being paid more. I lost a couple of orders, but my books were still full.

The ones I lost were the ones who thought that days of my

time were worth the same price as a supermarket cake and I decided I couldn't compete with them so I wasn't going to bother trying. Running a bespoke, creative business is hard. Pricing it is even harder. But once you've got it sorted you'll be fine.

I advise making a pricing guide and sticking to it.

Using my method above, I worked out how much I would charge for a basic 6" round, 7" round all the way up to a 16" round. I did the same for a square and I did the same for a fruit cake, (these ingredients usually end up costing a great deal more, with the addition of marzipan so I recommend pricing fruit cakes separately to sponge cakes). This way I knew what my prices started at and what my minimum cost for a basic cake was. When I say, '*started at*', it's because the price we are working out for your pricing guide is just for the cake itself.

For example, if someone ordered a cake from you with just a 'Happy Birthday' message on it and a pretty ribbon, then someone else ordered the same size cake but with two, personalised 3D models of the birthday girl and her cat, a message, small models of her favourite things as well as piped details around the cake and a specific flavour that you will have to buy specialist ingredients for, you simply can't charge the same amount. They may be two of the same size and therefore fall under the same bracket on your pricing guide, but they will be completely different levels of work and costings.

What I would do in this situation, is start with your pricing guide cake cost for that size cake, then add on costs for modelling and extra ingredients. You can do this either by pricing per model, again work out your ingredients costs first to see how much it will cost you to make, then add your time, or you can charge for modelling per hour. It's up to you.

By taking the time to work out a pricing chart and strategy to know what your cakes start at, it will make your life easier. It also makes tiered cakes easier to price as you can add up each cake and add on the extra costs for dowels and small cake boards etc. I would have a set charge added to tiered cakes to cover this so when working out the starting cost, I would add up the two sizes for example a 9" round cake plus a 7" round cake then add my 'tiered cake' cost and that price would be the starting rate. Once I had this figured I would then add the cost of my time, models, details etc.

Sculpted and "Fake Cakes"

Now you've got a pricing strategy for round and square cakes, what about something a little different? What if someone wants a 3D sculpted Mini Cooper Cake? A hand carved shaped cake will take a lot more time and therefore cost more. It doesn't matter if the customer asks for it to serve 10 people or 100 people, the process of costing these cakes should still be the same.

Firstly, work out how much cake you will need to bake, then add on your time to sculpt and decorate. In my opinion, sculpted cakes are best to price individually by design rather than by size of cake baked as they can differ so much. My starting price for sculpted cakes was always higher than my starting price for the same size standard cake. Once you've done a few sculpted cakes you will get a better idea of how long they take you, how much 'waste' you've got left over once you carve a cake and this should give you a better indication of how much to charge.

"Fake Cakes" can also be a costing conundrum. These are polystyrene dummies in the shape of round or square cakes, iced to look like a real cake. They are popular with weddings and events where the customer wants a large 'statement' cake but to serve fewer portions. As far as the customer will see it, it may be cheaper because you're not actually baking them a cake. But we now know, ingredients for the baking alone aren't the major factor in pricing.

I would price fake cakes at the same cost as baked cakes. This was for several reasons: You will need to buy the polystyrene fake cake in. Usually this will cost the same, if not more than baking the cake itself. You can buy these in a range of sizes and shapes from online cake stores.

You will still need to buy all the icing and boards to use on this cake. It will be the same amount of icing to cover it and I would still recommend buying a thin board to go underneath it. Whilst you don't need this for the same hygiene reasons as a normal cake, it still makes life easier when covering it in icing.

You will still need to decorate this cake and that will take the same time as a baked one. Even it's a plain tier at the bottom, it will still need to be iced and smoothed and 'cared for' like a normal cake.

I've done quite a few fake cakes over the years. For display cakes for a stand I held at a wedding fair, for a corporate function that wanted a 5-tier cake to mark their 5-year anniversary but only had about 40 people coming, a Halloween party centrepiece. There are lots of reasons you may be asked to make a fake cake, but just remember to price accordingly based on the ingredients and of course, your time.

As I have said, pricing is a very personal thing and I've seen it cause many an argument. I can tell you from personal experience that my prices soon changed after a few months of not charging enough. I'm not saying you go mad and start charging £500 for a single 8" round cake, unless that cake is covered in actual edible gold or something. Your prices still need to be affordable to your clients. There's no point pricing yourself so high you get no work at all, but I am encouraging you to have the confidence to charge what you're worth.

A home baker will never be able to compete with an £8 supermarket cake and nor should you. There will be plenty of people who will buy from you rather than buying from a store because they want a bespoke, custom, home baked, hand-made, tasty cake.

Character Cakes

Something I wanted to briefly touch on that I think you need to be aware of are character cakes. I get a lot of people ask me what the law is around these cakes as there is a lot of conflicting advice online.

If you buy and use an already licensed Disney or other brand character made from plastic to use on top of a decorated cake for a customer, I am under the impression this is fine as you have paid a 'copyright fee' but is still labelled as a grey area. However, if you make a cake or model of a trademarked or copyrighted character exactly, you can be at risk of copyright infringement.

There was a story that hit the press in America in 2015, of a baker being sued by representatives of Disney and Sanrio for, *"unlicensed and counterfeit edible cake frosting sheets and related items, which incorporate unauthorised likenesses of animated or live-action characters or other logos."* Closer to home was a story of a UK baker being fined £1000 by a large American corporation for recreating a copyrighted character out of sugar-paste for a cake topper. So, the threat is real.

For years it has been a subject of debate with the consensus being that the odds of being found out for copying an image are so small that many do it with the hopes of 'getting away with it'. Strictly speaking however, it is illegal to replicate a copyrighted image or figure without getting permission to do so first. That said, I can't tell you what decisions to make and how you will make those decisions in the interests of your business.

I know many bakers who do character cakes still and many who now refuse to do character cakes all together unless they are adding on licensed figures. There have been talks that companies like Disney are employing people to physically search and seek out businesses on the internet who are reproducing their characters without permission. I don't know how true this is but given the rise of 'cease and desist' letters I have seen sent out to bakers in recent years, it's really something to think about.

I'm not an expert in copyright so I can't give you a definitive answer but I will advise you to do your own research on the matter. There are literally hundreds of articles, blogs and pages available to read at your leisure online that go into much more depth and detail about copyrighted cakes, the laws surrounding them and ways you can obtain permission. What you decide to do upon reading all of this is up to you.

Dealing With Customers

It's all well and good having your auntie call you and say, "Can you just make a quick chocolate cake for Alfie's birthday this weekend? There's 10 of us. Pop a little bear on top too, cheers love." And taking that as an order, but when you are dealing with people outside of your family, I recommend a slightly different approach.

Usually I would take cake orders anywhere from a week in advance up to a year in advance, (mostly wedding cakes). Sometimes if people messaged me with super last-minute orders, if I could fit them in and I had in everything they needed, I would accept the order but would ask for payment in full, there and then, just to ensure you don't lose out.

For all cake orders, I recommend *taking a deposit*. Should the booking be cancelled for whatever reason, you don't want to be out of pocket if you have already paid out for the ingredients or specialist equipment. This fortunately only happened to me once as I didn't take deposits when I started. I had made the cake, a rainbow sponge with modelled figures on top, personalised for the birthday boy. I awaited collection at the agreed time and no one showed up. I called the lady who had ordered the cake and received back a text message simply saying "Don't need the cake anymore. Thanks".

I was devastated. I felt like all my hard work was for nothing and I felt completely under appreciated. From then on, I took deposits.

Then, later as my business grew and I became busier, I had a two-week notice period on *all* cake orders. I would also require a 50% deposit, with the other 50% to be paid on collection or delivery. Or if the customer was paying by BACS, Paypal or other digital means, the full balance to be paid 24 hours before collection or delivery. I had the same process with wedding cakes but slightly different figures which I go over in the next chapter.

Earlier when I spoke about logos and stationery and the like, I mentioned you can buy cake order pads. I absolutely loved these. They have spaces for you to put all contact details, cake details and additional information. It usually comes on a pad that provides you with a duplicate of the order for the customer to take away so if they spot something that isn't right after they leave, they can give you a call and you can sort things out.

If you don't have the budget for this sort of stationery, a normal pen and paper will do, but I do advise photocopying it or writing on a carbon copy notebook to ensure you and your customer both have a copy of the order.

You could include information such as:

Your business name and contact details including phone number.

The customer's name and contact details including phone number (if someone else other than the customer is ordering or collecting the cake, I would advise getting their contact number as well in case of any problems on the day).

The date and time of collection or delivery (if delivery, make sure to have a confirmed address of the venue and confirmation of time you will be able to get into the venue to drop the cake off or set it up).

The size and shape of cake. How many servings? If you've not yet got the hang of size to servings, there's a few great charts available online you can download and keep to-hand in your kitchen. There's one by *Iced Jems* that I use and love!

The flavours and fillings of the cake they have ordered. This only went wrong for me once. I made a cake, luckily for a friend, and it had been a busy week as I was still working two jobs at this point. They collected their cake and all seemed well. The next day she called me to tell me the cake was beautiful and delicious and perfect but, "I really thought I ordered lemon and not chocolate!".

I checked the text from her and she was right, it was meant to be lemon and I had provided them with a triple chocolate cake with chocolate buttercream, no lemon in sight! I was so embarrassed. Luckily, she and her guests didn't seem to mind but if this wasn't an understanding friend, it could have been a lot worse!

Any exact colours. When it comes to anything with design, just writing 'blue' isn't exceptionally helpful and when you look back at your notes can cause ambiguity. Delivering a cake that's sky blue when it's meant to be dark TARDIS blue for a Doctor Who party is *really* important. It's helpful to have colour samples attached to the order such as pictures or ribbon.

Allergy information. I don't need to stress just how important this is, but I will anyway. *This is important.* If someone has a very bad allergy, it can be life threatening. Be aware and write it down.

Dietary information. Such as if the cake is dairy free, gluten free, vegan. This information is just as important as allergens. Intolerances, whilst not usually life threatening, can still make someone very sick.

The message or greeting on the cake. Make sure this is checked and double checked. You don't want to get Emelia's name wrong on her birthday.

I have a friend who, whenever they see a picture of a cake I've made with a message on it, asks why I've spelt "Brithday" that way just to mess with me. I have got it wrong once too, on an order. I spelt Congratulations without the U. I can spell, I swear, but we all have off days. I quickly took the letters off and started again. You couldn't notice when I was finished but it's just a reminder to triple check the message before letting the cake leave. This is another reason why I will make sure a cake is finished a day before it's being collected or delivered; contingency and correction time.

The agreed price of the cake and, if a deposit is being paid, how much has been paid, what the outstanding balance is and when it is due and the customers signature to confirm they agree to the financial details. Again, if payment or part payment is made digitally, make sure to send over an email or text confirmation.

103

It's also useful to have some terms and conditions ready for your customers. These can be at the bottom of the order form or on a separate piece of paper all together. I would have mine signed by the customer and stapled to the back of their order.

It usually has information about deposits, refunds, cancellations, changes in the order, safety after collection, that kind of thing. For example, if they cancel a week before, or even a day before, are they eligible for a refund? Are they able to transfer their money to another occasion a few months away? When is the cut off point for any changes to be made to the cake? (I had someone call me the day before they were due to collect the cake to ask if it was too late to change the colour of the icing).

It's best to get all of this agreed now rather than further down the line. I have included with this book, a sample cake contract along with terms and conditions. This is a great starting point! Feel free to make your own and customise it as you see fit. Everyone will have a different way of running their business. I also recommend a disclaimer form for the customer to sign when the cake has been collected/delivered to agree it is all as expected and there are no issues. I have included an example of this too.

As you will be in the business of dealing with your customers face to face, there may be occasions where the customer isn't 100% happy. Now, this won't happen a lot, but it's good to know what to do in case it does.

An example I can remember is a time when a friend of mine made a three tier 'topsy turvy' wedding cake. It was collected without issue and was perfect. The customer checked the cake, loved it and then carried it to their car to drive back home. When the customer had got back, my baker friend received a phone call saying the cake was ruined! Confused, she asked the customer to send her a photo and lo and behold, the top tier had slid off and the bottom one had started to crack and crumble.

The cake was fine and sturdy when it was collected but some-how in the journey it had been damaged. The best guess we had was the customer, instead of putting the cake in the foot-well or boot on a flat surface as advised by the baker, put the cake on the seat. The angle of the seat combined with the bumping of driving on most British roads meant the cake was put under un-necessary pressure. Although we couldn't prove this was how the damage had occurred, it was just our best guess.

Now, technically the cake was fine when it left the baker's kit-chen, but she had no proof of this. The customer tried to say it was damaged to a certain extent when they collected it. If my baker friend had the customer sign a terms and conditions and collection form, she would have had this as evidence to back up her claim that it wasn't. Regardless, she did what every good business person does, and something I highly recommend to also do, she fixed it. She asked the customer to bring the cake back and she put it back together again.

In the end, you wouldn't have noticed a difference. The baker didn't have to do that, she wasn't obligated to in any way. However, by doing the right thing and going out of her way, the couple were thrilled with the cake and the day went smoothly. As a result, the baker got many more bookings from the wedding.

Please remember: your reputation is *everything*. If something bad should happen, - say a cake isn't fully cooked, something is spelled wrong, or even the colour scheme isn't what the customer is expecting - go out of your way to make it right, even if you don't believe you are in the wrong. Put pride aside and get on with it.

The last thing you need as a new business is for a customer to bad mouth you to their friends. We are far more likely to tell people about a negative experience than we are about a positive one. Sometimes, even a botched cake can lead to a positive review if your customer service is good. We *all* make mistakes but it's how we put them right that's the important thing.

Wedding Cakes

I felt like wedding cakes should have their own chapter because they really feel like a completely different animal. They shouldn't, I mean, it's the same kind of ingredients, same sort of work but something about them just feels different. There's a different kind of pressure that comes with making someone's wedding cake that you don't feel when making a box of birthday cupcakes. I'm not saying the latter is any less important, but what I am saying is wedding cakes come with their own problems and difficulties that need addressing.

For the first few years that I was making cakes for people, I didn't take on any wedding cake orders. I could have, I had the space in my diary and I needed the work, but I specifically didn't take them on because I didn't think I could handle them; and that's completely ok. I didn't want the pressure on my shoulders that I could 'make or break' a wedding day.

I knew I could decorate cakes quite well and my friends always seemed happy with the orders I had made for them, but I didn't feel ready for an ivory tiered centrepiece that hundreds of people would see and the happy couple would have photos of for years to come.

It didn't make me any less of a cake decorator, it made me a realist. I needed more practice before I was at that level. I know that these criticisms were coming from me and my rather high standards, but it was a feeling I didn't want to ignore.

There are a few things I think all beginner business bakers should know before embarking on their first paid wedding cake.

Are you ready? This isn't meant to be a patronising comment in any way. This is a completely honest question. We've all seen the news articles 'I paid hundreds of pounds for a wedding cake that collapsed and ruined my day!' and the compilation posts of 'Wedding cake fails!'. I would have nightmares that my first wedding cake would end up on a website like Buzzfeed for all the wrong reasons. Only you will know what level you are at in your cake baking journey.

Can you do what the couple have asked for? There is a famous saying by Richard Branson; *'If somebody offers you an amazing opportunity but you are not sure you can do it, say yes – then learn how to do it later!'* and I agree with this to a certain extent. However, if the betrothed couple have asked for a 3D carved cake, 6 tiers high with lights and music and 40 personalised models, 10 different flavours to feed 400 people and you don't feel comfortable doing any of these things, or that you can't learn how to do these things in confidence by the time the cake is due, there is little point in saying yes and then getting completely stressed out, feeling overwhelmed and fraught.

If the cake is booked far in advance, which most wedding cakes usually are, and you have time to practice in between booking and when the cake is due then by all means, take the booking, go out of your comfort zone and smash your targets - I believe in you! But, if you are doubtful of any aspect of the cake, be honest, with both the couple and yourself.

I, personally know that my people modelling (specifically standing people) isn't the best. I can model a lion and a giraffe well. I rather like doing animals, but standing people have never been my strong point.

If I had practiced them and spent time on them, I'm completely confident that in time my people modelling skills would have gone from strength to strength. But as it was, I never took on a wedding cake with a standing people topper because I wasn't totally sure they would look as the couple wanted and you really want to go for the 'wow!' factor with cakes, not the 'oh...' factor. But if you wanted a giraffe and a lion in wedding outfits, I'm your girl.

Can you fit it in? Time is a funny thing when it comes to baking. It just disappears. You work it out in your head 'ok, a few hours baking, a few hours decorating, I can easily fit this in!' but, it usually takes longer than you think it's going to, especially when you work from home. If you've got other people in the house, they can alter your schedule accidentally. If anything goes wrong and you've got to rectify it, that also adds time on to your working day and so forth. I would always estimate how long a project would take me and usually add on an hour or two just to be on the safe side.

I would much rather be ahead of schedule than working gone midnight (which has happened on more than a few occasions!).

Wedding cakes, much like the TARDIS in '*Doctor Who*', work through time in their own way, especially when you're quite new to them. You have the added pressure to get it 'perfect', so you naturally take your time with it and you spend more time 'faffing' with it once it's completed as you will always see any little thing you just need to change before the couple comes to collect or you are ready to deliver the cake.

When I started taking wedding cakes as orders, I made sure it was the only cake order I had on that week. I could have fitted in more, but I wanted to be sure I could dedicate all my time to it. By the end, when I was happy and comfortable in my kitchen and business, I would take on a couple of wedding cakes and occasion cakes, and even some cupcakes in one week, knowing I would be able to complete them all with little concern. But remember, it's YOUR business and you can run it exactly as you like.

If you're reading this thinking 'Britt, this isn't my first day at the rodeo, I've made many wedding cakes for friends before now and I know what I'm doing!' then that's awesome, but I do know for me especially, the idea of wedding cakes was quite daunting so I wanted to go into some detail for the new business bakers reading this book.

Consultations

Ok, so you've decided to add wedding cakes to your repertoire. You've had a few successful practises and you're ready to meet with the happy couple. One brilliant way of securing a wedding cake booking is by doing consultations. These are usually a short meeting with the engaged couple to discuss wedding cake options, designs and flavours.

Usually, you will make samples for the couple to taste. This can be done in a few ways. If you have more than one consultation booked in on the same day, you can make several small cakes in your best flavours, cut them up into slices and individually wrap them to keep them fresh.

Another way is to make different flavoured cupcakes for the couple to share and try. However you do it, I recommend choosing flavours that you're confident in baking, ones you've maybe had compliments on in the past, a fun and 'different' selection as well as some traditional options.

When I did a consultation, I would usually make a vanilla, chocolate, lemon, salted caramel, red velvet, coconut and lime, raspberry and white chocolate and nan's favourite; fruit cake. What you do and make is completely up to you. Don't feel tied to any one thing because of 'tradition' as you may get a completely untraditional couple. I think in all the wedding cakes I've made, only one of them has had a fruit cake tier.

One thing to have on hand during a consultation is your portfolio. I bought a nice presentation booklet from a stationery shop and I filled it with printed out pictures of my previous cakes and bakes. I then moved on to a slideshow on my laptop to show them. This is an opportunity to show off your talents and give the couple an idea of your style of decorating.

It sounds obvious but if you're doing the consultation at home, make sure there is somewhere nice and tidy for them to sit. Offer them a beverage and present the samples on nice plates with little cake forks. The little touches really go a long way and the fact is, it's their wedding day and they deserve to have the special treatment.

One couple I had, referred by a friend so they didn't know me personally, also asked to see my kitchen, which is fair enough if you are catering for them and their friends and loved ones, so be prepared for that too. Make sure you've got a notebook to record their thoughts and designs and have your pricing structure to hand as this will really help.

Most consultations I did, I emailed the couple within 24 hours with a detailed quote comprising of; the chosen design, flavours, how many it had to feed, collection/delivery date, address and time. I would also include any other facts I thought necessary such as the topper to add to the cake, or any personal items such as ribbon and health and safety advice like how many dowels would be included if it was a tiered cake and so forth. It's best to get everything in writing at this stage and agreed to in writing also, in case there are any discrepancies later.

Once the couple have confirmed the booking I highly recommend getting a deposit. Slightly differently to other occasion cakes which I spoke about in the previous chapter, for wedding cakes, I would usually take a 25% deposit to secure the booking date and then the rest paid in full two weeks before the wedding. I would generally take less of a deposit as wedding cakes can be more expensive than your every-day birthday cake and this way makes it easier to pay.

Most wedding cakes I made however, were paid in full a few months before when all the finances were being settled, but it's good to have a cut-off point. I would do it this way to completely cover myself as the bigger the cake, (as wedding cakes generally are), the more money you will be spending on ingredients, icing and equipment and you don't want to ever be out of pocket for an order. A wedding cake is usually collected the night before the wedding or the morning of and final settlement of the cake bill can easily be forgotten in the excitement of the day. *Make sure to cover yourself.*

You may not do a consultation at all. Some couples know exactly what they want when they are looking for a cake maker and that's great. They may have gone to an event you baked for previously and already know what your cakes taste like.

No matter how you get the booking, consultation or not, be advised that most wedding cakes will be booked 6-9 months before the wedding. Get yourself a diary for the following year when they become available for exactly this reason.

The last thing you want to do is to take a booking for months and months in advance and then only realise the week of the wedding or worse, have it slip your mind all together. This is extreme and rather rare I know, but a lot of bakers I know, myself included, have muddled up dates from time to time. We're all human.

The best thing you can do is cover yourself for every eventuality.

How Much To Charge?

I go into much more detail on how much to charge for your cakes in a previous chapter of this book, however wedding cakes again, are slightly different. They will usually be the biggest cakes you do, (although that said I did make a Christening cake once that was bigger than any wedding cake I made! So, it's not set in stone) and you need to charge accordingly. I'm not saying for one second that just because it's got the word 'wedding' attached to it you should hike the price up, I don't agree with that at all. What I am saying is to consider how long each component will take you and make sure you are compensated. I know we bake for the love of it but this is still a business.

The average wedding cake in the UK in 2016 cost £300 and with the rise of more brides wanting to make their own wedding cake and supermarkets like M&S having a bridal range, it's a very competitive market these days. As a home baker, you cannot compete with the big supermarket chains, and nor should you, so please don't try. I have seen cake makers fighting and haggling on certain social media selling pages, undercutting each other to secure the booking. You don't need to do this. Stick to your pricing structure, keep being you and the orders will come.

Wedding Fairs

Wedding fairs are a great way to market yourself and to meet prospective couples. I have found in my experience that they are usually more expensive to have a table at than say a farmer's market or craft fair and you will need to have some wedding cakes to show, (I recommend polystyrene dummy cakes), and even possibly cakes to taste, so understandably this is for when you have a defined advertising budget. But by doing just one of these fairs you could fill up your diary for the whole wedding season. If wedding cakes are a route you want to take it may be worth doing one of these so you can meet the couples in person and charm them with your cakes! Then you can book in a date for a free wedding consultation.

Local Wedding Advertising

A jeweller local to me always has a lovely decorated, (I'm assuming polystyrene,) wedding cake in the window of the shop, next to the wedding rings. It also has business cards next to it of the person who made the cake. This is a brilliant bit of wedding advertising that came about all down to a conversation. The people going to the jewellers looking at wedding rings will very probably need a cake and there's one right in front of them! It is always worth asking local companies if they will display your cakes with your contact information. You could always offer a referral percentage to sweeten the deal. The worst they can say is 'no'.

Great places to try are jewellers, wedding dress boutiques, suit shops, venues and florists. Good people to talk to as well are photographers and wedding planners. Introduce yourself, bring some cake, have a few conversations and they may refer out to you.

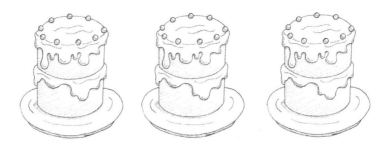

Timeline Of A Cake

How long does it take to make a cake? As the famous saying goes; How long is a piece of string?

I used to really struggle with my time management, especially if I had more than one cake on the go. I would make and decorate the cake super last minute, not because I wasn't organised, but I thought that if I made the cake more than 24 hours before it was being collected, it wouldn't be fresh enough for the customer.

It was about three months into taking orders and being up until 2am when I conceded that something had to change. I had a look at the recipe I was using at the time, a Victoria sponge which doesn't have a very long shelf life, and looked to change it so it stayed fresher for longer and gave me more time. The amount of times I would be rushing to have a cake finished before the customer came around was getting silly and the panic and anxiety of it all was keeping me awake at night.

Over the years, I developed what I now refer to as my 'Cake Timeline'. It made my life so much easier and allowed me to take more orders during a week without killing me, which in turn made me more profit and a more successful business. The most popular day for cake collections was a Saturday so I usually worked backwards from there. Now, the longevity of each cake will very much depend on the recipe but I wanted to take you through my normal week when I was baking commission cakes for customers.

Please note, this timeline isn't suitable for cupcakes. Whilst you can make your decorations quite far in advance, I wouldn't recommend baking cupcakes longer than 2-3 days before they will be enjoyed, as they don't have a layer of icing keeping them fresh on the inside, they dry out very quickly!

Recipe

A recipe which lasts well is a great place to start. Something like a carrot cake or a Victoria sponge is only going to last you a couple of days so you don't have a lot of time for decorating. I highly recommend, and have used hundreds and hundreds of times, a madeira cake for a decorated celebration cake. They are very easy to adapt to any flavour you like and a classic vanilla with raspberry jam and vanilla buttercream just screams 'birthday cake' to me!

You can find the recipe I use and tips on how to scale up and down, as well as my vanilla buttercream recipe on my website. Once baked and cooled, a madeira cake will last two weeks and freeze for three months.

With regards to filings, if it's a cake you're going to finish decorating in advance, I recommend a buttercream or ganache as these last well not refrigerated, however, a cream cheese frosting or fresh cream filling will need to be kept cool, so just be aware of this.

Once the cake is baked and cooled, wrap it tightly in cling film until you are ready to split, fill and cover it. I'll be going through that below but for now, know you can keep it wrapped in tight cling-film for several days before doing anything with it. It's at this wrapped stage you can cover it in a layer of foil and freeze if needed (see below). Do not be tempted to store the cake in the fridge however. This will dry the cake out and affect the taste. It doesn't need to go in there! Say I'm making a cake for a weekend celebration, this is the day by day run of what I would do.

Monday

Monday is my baking day! I bake all the cakes needed for the week and then leave them to cool upside down on greaseproof paper, (not a cooling rack), and when completely cold, I wrap them tightly in cling film. Then I leave them in a cool, dry room upside down until I'm ready to decorate.

Tuesday

Tuesday is when I will make the filling (buttercream, ganache etc.) and split and fill my cakes as I tend to make them in one deep tin rather than a few separate sandwich tins. If I am carving my cakes, I would do this now. Then I will stick the cake to a thin cake card with a little buttercream. I crumb coat them, (cover in a layer of buttercream/ganache) and then cover in a layer of sugar-paste/icing. I'll then smooth them and sharpen the edges and leave alone overnight for the icing to set. It is also today I will ice the board.

Note. If I am icing a fruit cake or putting on a layer of marzipan first, I would do this today and leave it overnight before covering in a layer of sugar-paste/icing. This gives you the best chance at nice smooth edges. It's hard to get smooth icing over soft marzipan, you need to leave it to firm up a bit. Also, if I am tiering my cakes, I'll leave the sugar-paste/icing to set overnight before doing anything else with them.

Wednesday

On a Wednesday, I start to make any decorations. Any models, cut out shapes, messages, anything I am decorating my cake with. I'll leave my decorations to dry on foam overnight. I find foam is better than kitchen roll or left on the side as it allows air to get all the way around the shape and dry nicely.

You can make your decorations much further in advance if you like, if you keep them in a box which air can get into but dust can't, (like a cake box for example), then they will last ages as sugar is a natural preservative. These also do not need to be kept in the fridge. If I have a spare rainy afternoon (which we get a lot of in England!) I will sit with the radio on and make all the decorations needed for the coming week's orders.

Don't store edible decorations in an airtight container like a cake tin or tupperware box as the sugar will start to 'sweat' and will go very soft. Not great for our decorations!

Today I also fix my iced cakes onto their iced boards with a little royal icing and I leave this to set before decorating. If I am tiering my cakes, now is when I will place in my dowels and stack the cake, sticking it together with royal icing. Again, I'll leave it to set completely.

If I'm icing a fruit cake, today is when I will cover it in a layer of sugar-paste/icing.

Thursday

Today is when I decorate my cakes! This is when it all starts to come together and starts to look awesome! Once all the decorations are

123

on, I leave them to dry and then photograph and box up my cakes. I then leave them in a cool, dry room. Again, not a fridge, especially once it's iced as the condensation when the cake comes back to room temperature afterwards will cause the icing to go damp.

Friday

Friday is my contingency day! Should I wake up and find my model has lost his head, (this has ACTUALLY happened more than once) or in a rush yesterday I have spelt Brithday wrong, today is the day I can put it right. Also, by giving myself an extra day, it means I can take on more work, be more productive and get more done.

It also means if necessary the customer can collect the cake Friday evening and the cake is good to go.

Saturday

Cake Day! Today is the day I found was most popular for customers to collect cakes, if they haven't done the night before, or the day of the event I have made the cake for.

I used to get so nervous when customers collected their cakes. Something I had spent hours on for their celebration they were going to see for the first time! Over the years there have been a few customer tears shed in my kitchen, luckily all happy ones!

Being a cake decorator is something really, very special and rewarding.

Once your cake has been cut into, you want to make sure no air gets to it to keep it fresh for as long as possible, so wrap with cling film and keep it in the cake box.

Sunday

If you're making the cake for yourself or your family, today is the day to eat leftover cake for breakfast! If it was for a customer, time to chill out and have a nice cup of tea (and maybe more cake?).

And there you have it! My week as a cake decorator. So, remember, there's no need to stay up until 3am the night before the birthday party to finish the cake (although, I will be the first to admit I have done this more than once!).

Use a good, stable recipe, plan ahead, take your time and you'll find the whole experience a lot less stressful and a lot more rewarding!

It goes without saying that of course, you can make a cake in less time than this, however I personally wouldn't recommend baking and decorating a cake in one day. The crumb structure will be too soft and you may find the whole process a lot harder than it needs to be. If you're really pushed for time then for a cake needed on a Saturday, you could bake on a Thursday, decorate on a Friday and then enjoy on the Saturday. This way the cake has 'settled', the icing is set and there is less chance of breakages in delivering/collection.

However, for tiered cakes I would always leave it at least overnight stacked before attempting to move it. As I've said, this is my method that has been very successful for me for many years. Everyone will have different ways of working that works best for them and I wanted to share mine with you all.

Freezing Cakes

Whether you want to bake in advance, have a TON of cakes to get baked or you've inadvertently made a cake on the wrong date (guilty!), freezing cakes and cupcakes can be a handy tool to add to your skill set and help you with time management. I used to keep a few popular sizes of cakes (8" round, 7" square for example) in my freezer for last minute orders.

It requires a little patience and preparation but can save you a lot of time in the long run allowing you to bake ahead of schedule, perfect for large orders, weddings and parties. Also, flash freezing fruit cakes is a quick way of 'maturing' it!

Well, the defrosting process is.

If I bake a fruit cake and don't have months to let it come to its best, a quick overnight trip to the freezer does the job!

You will be able to freeze most cakes. I find that Madeira cakes (and their chocolate and lemon counterparts) freeze wonderfully without too much hassle, as do most cakes with a high fat content. It is very important that once your cakes are baked, you leave them to *cool completely*. If they are still warm this will create condensation which can cause cakes to get the dreaded 'soggy bottom'.

Once they are cooled, it's also important to wrap them well, otherwise they may get very dry when frozen (freezer burn isn't tasty), which isn't what we want. I find the best way to do this for sponge cakes is two layers of cling film and then a tight layer of foil. However, for fruit cakes, I tend to use two layers of greaseproof paper and then a tight layer of foil.

It's also ideal to briefly freeze cakes that you plan to carve, mainly because the crumb structure is more solid so it will keep its shape better and there's less chance of it crumbling when shaping and crumb coating.

If you are freezing cupcakes, firstly make sure to bake them in greaseproof or foil cases as this will prevent the dreaded peeling cases when you defrost them, then pop them in a sandwich bag and make sure they have enough space on the freezer shelf and they aren't squashed.

Here's a few key hints and tips that will help you chill your bakes:

❖ *Freeze naked!* I find to get best results, freeze cakes and cupcakes un-iced and before you split them to fill them. This will stop them going dry and stops any frosting and icing 'sweating' over your cake when it's defrosting.

❖ Take your cake or cupcakes out of the freezer a few hours (preferably overnight) before you plan to decorate them. This will ensure they have fully defrosted.

❖ To defrost, leave on the kitchen side and not in the fridge. Also, I take off the layer of tin foil but leave it wrapped in cling film.

❖ Make sure they are fully defrosted before decorating as again, this can also cause condensation and promote mould growth.

❖ Don't freeze for longer than three months. Everything has a shelf life and I find if you leave it longer than this, the cake is simply past its peak; any time before this will taste fine, however.

❖ Label and date your cakes. This is good practice for all food health and hygiene and imperative when running a business. Pop on a little sticker saying what it is and when you put it in.

❖ Putting your cake back in the tin once wrapped then putting the whole thing in the freezer can help it keep its shape if you've got quite a 'busy' freezer.

Does a frozen cake taste different? I honestly would say no. I've tried all manner of cake over the years and I have never been able to taste a difference if a cake has been frozen or not, some argue that it makes it taste better! If you're unsure, give it a practice run. Any excuse to enjoy a slice of cake!

Let's Get Personal

Let's get real personal for a minute. We've sorted through the practical elements of starting a cake business from home, all the admin and the 'official' stuff, but one thing that's worth mentioning is not to take things personally in business. By this I mean, when you sit and take your time to calculate how much you want to charge for your cakes, it won't be in everyone's budget - and that's ok. But something which used to upset me and the statement I know a lot of my fellow bakers get, is *But it's just a cake?!'*

What the average, non-baker or occasional hobby baker won't realise is how much time, energy and love you have spent to create their special cake. They may not necessarily be aware that making a handmade, bespoke centrepiece for their occasion will cost more than an off the shelf supermarket offering. Now, supermarket cakes certainly have their place, (hands up who has ever enjoyed a Colin Caterpillar?), and I am not putting down supermarket cakes in ANY WAY, nor am I saying anything negative about those who buy them.

Before I started baking, my local supermarket was my first port of call on anyone's birthday, BUT what I am saying is they have no place being compared to a completely personal, home baked cake. They are two separate entities. That said, some people will still compare your cakes to those found in a supermarket. Some people will struggle to understand why a shop can charge £8 for a cake and you are charging more. They will think it's just flour and eggs. You will know it's not.

What these people forget is the cost of the tools, the price of equipment, your experience, the cost and length of any training or classes you do to perfect your craft and most importantly, your time! Some people will want you to work for much less than they would be willing to accept for themselves.

I once had someone ask me for a quote on a cake, which upon looking at the photo before doing any calculations I knew it would be at least £60, but they had added 'I don't want to spend more than £25' at the bottom of their message.

For that price, I worked out that I would be working for less than £1 per hour.

This was a 'friend' of mine who had asked me and I was frankly, insulted. I explained to her how much the materials would cost, then how much time it would take me and added on the very, very low profit (less than £1) I would be making from said cake to which she replied, 'but it's your hobby, you enjoy it don't you?'. She had assumed because it was something I enjoyed doing, I would be happy to lose money simply for the joy of making a cake. Some people are happy to do that, but they don't last too long in business by doing so.

There are also those in the camp of 'well if I buy you the ingredients can you make it?'. Again, these people do not see your time as being valuable and that can be upsetting but it's up to you how you handle it.

I now know that the reason people ask questions like these is simply down to a lack of understanding of the process and how long it takes. I find by explaining to these people that it would take me X hours to turn those raw ingredients into a special cake for Harry's birthday, they realise a little more how much work is involved.

You may also get the 'I'll just make it myself' response. One of two things will happen in the days that follow that statement, they will enjoy making the cake so much you will have a new fully-fledged cake decorator friend, OR, they will realise it's much harder than it looks and it's much more than just a few ingredients. Then you will have gained a customer when they save themselves the hassle and order from you next time around.

Most of the time too, when people ask for a price or you send them a quote, they won't even get back to you to say thank you. I think they assume you have every eventuality of cake cost already figured out, when you've just spent 20 minutes or so figuring out the sizes, ingredients, costing of models and equipment to provide them with a bespoke cost only to get radio silence in return. This may seem rude, but try not to let it get to you.

A request I used to get quite often, was "can I order a cake for tomorrow morning please?" and nine times out of ten I would get this message when I was sitting down for my dinner. I used to think 'sure, I'll just fire up my magic time travelling oven and start on that a few days ago for you'. I can make some awesome things out of sugar, if I do say so myself, but I can't perform miracles.

I know bakers who have received messages like that and stayed up half the night trying to make it, only to be knackered the following day having not done their best work and ultimately regretting the decision. It was always one I would turn down and kindly explain I need at least five days' notice, preferably two weeks or more, for any cake order.

Free cake anyone?

It may surprise you to know that when I was making commission cakes weekly, (and still occasionally nowadays), I would get multiple requests a month for free cakes. Either for a charity or an event or my personal favourite, *'promotional purposes'*. How you handle these requests is up to you.

For example, I would have allocated time and resources set aside for certain charity work I would want to do, such as Macmillan Coffee Mornings, Cancer Research events, Depressed Cake Shop pop ups as these causes are close to my heart. Outside of this, I did turn down a lot of charity requests, which at the beginning made me feel bad, I must admit, as I hated saying no, (still do…), but I simply didn't have the time to fit them in and I didn't want my paid work to suffer as a result. My customers came first. But if you want to do lots of them, a few of them, none of them, it's completely up to you. Just don't overstretch yourself.

Event requests were a funny one. I had a well-known local business expo get in contact with me asking for 200 cupcakes, various flavours and colours, with the logo of the event made from edible paper on the top. I emailed them back with a quote to which they replied they 'didn't have the budget for the cakes' and hoped I would do it in exchange for a ticket to the event and to have my business cards (about 2000 of them, which I would need to buy of course) put in the goody bags. It would have cost me a lot of money to provide the event with that many cakes and business cards, more than I had in my advertising budget, so I turned it down.

Having a 'free cake advertising allowance' specifically for promotion can be a good idea, word of mouth and people tasting your cakes, are a great way to get the word out, but don't let people take advantage of your good nature.

A story that had recently come out was a baker being asked to make free cakes for both a reality TV 'star' and a reality TV singing competition. They had asked the baker to make both cakes in exchange for 'promotion' but it was unclear as to what the promotion would be exactly. I personally believe they were asking simply to get something for free, rather than having the baker's best interests at heart. The baker not only replied politely turning down the requests, but also posted their messages online so people got a better understanding of the kind of messages creative businesses get regularly. ...*Good on her I say.*

I did quite a few free 'promotional' cakes in the first year (aside from the charity cakes I like to do). Mostly cupcakes for events. Some paid off and I got one or two orders from it, and some didn't and I lost money. As with most things in life and business, it's a bit of a gamble and ultimately a decision only you can make. Try to assess how many people will be going, if you can have business cards or flyers right next to the cakes, and if you can attend to be there to meet the people enjoying your bakes. Under the right circumstances it can be quite lucrative for you.

You may also get family and friends expecting you to make cakes for free. How you handle this one is your choice. I've made cakes for friends and loved ones as birthday or wedding presents before now. I've also had friends order cakes from me and pay full price, even when I've tried to give them a discount. I've even had friends asking me to make a cake in return for a bottle of vodka (I'm a spirit girl, I don't drink wine... *don't judge me*). It all depends what you want to do.

I'll be honest, when I had people questioning my costs or people asking for free cakes every other day, it was hard not to take things to heart. I knew the base costs of what I had to charge as I was running a business, and not a charity and for 95% of those who got in contact with me, they knew, respected, and understood this. But there will be 5% of people who will challenge your business. I just want to add, I wasn't the most expensive cake decorator in Kent, I was nowhere near that! I wasn't the cheapest either, I sat somewhere in the middle.

You must keep strong, hold your head up and stick to your guns. It's not a reflection on you. Believe in yourself, you got this.

You WILL get people asking you to make a four tier, personalised themed cake with handmade models of all the characters for tomorrow morning and they only want to spend £25.

You can deal with this how you like, but don't for one second think it's anything to do with you or your work. They simply don't know how much time and effort is involved in the cake baking and making process.

People will try to get something for nothing (hell, we ALL do it) but please don't take it personally.

Practice, Practice, Practice

As with everything in life, the more you do something, the better you are at it. When I first started baking cakes, I wasn't very good. I'll be the first to admit that. But, I had very supportive friends who wanted to help me in my new business venture and so, they and their contacts ordered cakes from me and I am forever grateful to them for giving me that confidence.

Looking back, I don't think I was ready to start taking orders at all, but I'm so glad I bit the bullet and just got on with it. It's only now, years later that I can look back at my first cakes with a bit of judgement, but a lot of love.

I can remember being so proud of my first ever cake, my Pudsey. He set off a chain reaction I had never anticipated. From making him that rainy November afternoon, to taking cake orders for friends, to running a full time baking business, to accepting my first award for my business, to teaching cake decorating classes and opening my own cake school, to becoming an international public speaker, to demonstrating on stage to hundreds of people, to writing recipes for some of the biggest baking brands and UK supermarkets, to having a multi award winning baking blog and website, to writing and publishing this book you are reading today. None of this would have happened if it wasn't for packet mix Pudsey. You don't know where this cake filled life is going to take you.

When I think about my first cake, he's not much to look at. A bit cracked, a bit sunken and a bit raw in the middle. But he started a journey for me. As the months turned to years, I learnt so many things. Mainly due to making the mistakes and learning from them.

I was never a natural baker or business woman, I had to learn all these new skills along the way. These days, there are a lot more options for learning, such as cake classes, online courses, business seminars, YouTube videos, magazines, demonstrations and lots more.

When I set up and started my cake decorating classes, I wanted to teach beginners all the little hints, tips and tricks to make professionally decorated cakes. These little nuggets of information weren't things I had been taught, but were ways I found worked best for me. So many things in that class took me years to figure out and I am happy to pass on my new knowledge.

That is how I have treated this book. I'm not saying this is the only way to start a cake business from home, but I am saying this is the way I did it, and quite successfully too I might add.

I firmly believe there is no right or wrong way to bake. So many people get taught by their family members, some in colleges, some from online classes. Some people bake all in one tin (me for one), some bake in two. Some people use butter, some use margarine. Some use branded products, some don't. Some bake at a high temperature, some at a low. It is completely up to you.

The mistake is made when you believe your way is the right and only way. I've never thought like this, in anything. It's one of the reasons I'm always keen to point out my flaws, through my stories of how I started *my* cake business from home.

Even if you only take some of these tips, all these tips, or none at all, you will still create a business and a brand to be proud of. I can only tell you about my experience and the choices and decisions that made *my* life easier.

I'm still learning myself, so much every day, about baking and business and life in general. The cake industry changes so quickly. Trends come and go in the blink of an eye. It wasn't that long ago it was ALL about royal icing. I watch YouTube videos, I buy magazines, I read books, I love learning.

I re-made my Pudsey cake on his fifth anniversary and used all the knowledge I had gained over the years. The little tips and hints to make cake decorating 'easier'. He looks so much better, so polished; how I wanted the original one to look, before I knew what I was doing.

If there are some elements of your cakes that you aren't happy with or you think need improving; ***practice, practice, practice***. Trust me, you won't be short of volunteers to help you get rid of the evidence!

Cake Life

Making cakes will change your life.

I'm not just saying that. Once you enter this sugar-coated world, things will change.

You might wake up at 3am with a brilliant idea for a cake design, *(make sure to keep a notebook and a pen by the bed for just such an occasion!)*. You will see everything as inspiration.

You will become obsessed with cakes, (more than you are now), and spend far too much money on equipment and tools. You will go to cake shows and get sucked into amazing demonstrations and buy products you'll only use once.

You will be asked by friends and family members what you think of the cake when you go to a wedding or party (I still get this one EVERY TIME! I mean what are they expecting me to say?). Hours will be spent watching baking shows on TV, cake decorating competitions, YouTube videos and tutorials and more.

There will be times your kitchen will be overrun with cakes when testing out new recipes and ideas. There will be cakes you find yourself desperate to make, designs you want to try.

You will become "the cake person" in social circles. "Oh! You're the baker, aren't you?" will be a familiar greeting. Brace yourself for the usual following of "Did you bring any cakes with you?".

At first this was cute, there are only so many times you can laugh and say, "Not this time!". You will rarely be seen without an apron on and your friends will now think you sleep in your kitchen. Everything you own will be covered in a thin layer of icing sugar.

You will make yourself cuppa after cuppa only for each one to go cold before you can finish it because you get sucked into **'Cake Time'**, a baking phenomenon that occurs when you are most busy and the hours go by like no time at all and you look up at the clock and see it's late.

It's not just your life that will change, but your family life too. If you have a partner, husband, wife, they need to be prepared.

Cakes are coming.

They will be sent out to the shop at all hours when you've run out of one pivotal ingredient you need, but you can't go get it yourself because you've got six cakes baking in the oven and a Little Mermaid model on the side you need to finish. They will become well versed in the cake lingo. They will know their cornflour from their icing sugar, their caster sugar from their granulated.

While you may feel guilty for asking their help, they love you and want to see you happy. So, yes, they will go to Sainsbury's at ten to midnight to pick you up half a dozen eggs when you need to redo cupcakes before the morning, (*thank you Tim!*) and they will return triumphant.

There will be hours, days, even weeks where all parts of the kitchen is off limits. Where, "no, I'm sorry you can't go make a sandwich or grab a biscuit, I have a wedding cake on the side" will be a common argument. Where you forget to make yourself dinner because you are so close (4 hours) away from finishing a project.

There will be cakes you simply aren't happy with. Where you can see every crack, bump and crease and you will feel like you aren't cut out for this job. There will be days where nothing goes right. Where every cake you bake doesn't come out perfect. Days where you can't get your icing smooth and your buttercream soft. Days where you wonder why you left your 9-5 in the first place.

There will be days when you want to quit.

I had only been running my business for two weeks and already handed in notice to myself three times. "THAT'S IT!" I cried. "I quit." My eyes welled up with tears, my hands shook with frustration. "I'm clearly not cut out for this. I can't do it." I opened my laptop and went to the CV uploading website I had visited the previous week. Once again, I start re-writing my resume with feelings of both disappointment and regret.

Before starting *She Who Bakes*, working a 9-5 admin role was what filled my days and baking and cake decorating for friends and family was just a hobby that filled my evenings. Well… took over my nights. "Another 2am finish" I had thought just a month prior, "Something's gotta give." And so, it did, I had taken the decision to leave the safety of full time employment and spread my entrepreneurial wings. The only trouble was, suddenly, everything was different. I was different.

There was added pressure on me to get this perfect. Now, if I made a mistake, my reputation was on the line. The last thing I wanted was to ruin my career before it had even started. Yet the tasks that had once been so simple to me were becoming problematic. "Calm down, Britt. Breathe." I said to myself as I re-baked the batch of vanilla cupcakes for the fourth time that evening.

The first batch had no sugar, I had simply forgotten to put it in. The second had cases peeling away and this time I had mistaken plain flour for self-raising and essentially made dry scones. Not the light and fluffy cupcakes expected for the Christening tomorrow.

"Vanilla cupcakes are a basic staple of a baker. If I can't get this right, what's the point in trying to run a business?" Talking out loud to myself.

In the time between handing in my notice at the 9-5 and that moment, my self-esteem, confidence and belief had hit an all-time low. The week before when I had decided to create a recipe for my new blog, I had mistaken 'pink lemonade concentrate' for just normal pink lemonade. I thought being creative would make me feel better. So, 24 hours after I left my pink lemonade cheesecake to set, I took it out of the fridge.

Serving plate and camera at the ready, I unclipped the tin and WHOOOOOSSSSSHHHHHH. Pink lemonade spilled out from the metal ring and covered the entire kitchen. I burst into tears. "I can't even get this right." I thought. "I have no business being in business."

I took a few days out. I walked, I wrote, I chilled. I went to the park to have a word with myself. "This is what you want to do. This is what makes you happy", I mused. I was taking every mistake as a personal failure. Each time I messed up, I sank deeper into doubt.

Then, I realised. I'm making mistakes BECAUSE I'm stressed out. I'm putting far too much pressure on myself. "That's what you must do though, isn't it?" I thought. When you are running your own business, the buck stops with you. Every mistake costs YOU money. If you aren't worried about it, you don't care, and if you don't care you don't make money. Right? Those thoughts spiralled so fast in my head. But it was those thoughts alone that caused me to slip.

I sat in the park and cried. I cried for so long in fact, I cried until I laughed. The reality was that I had two options, give up before I'd even begun and get a 'proper job' or give it another go. I couldn't walk away from it. Not now. "You've sacrificed so much to get here" I thought, "don't quit."

So, I dusted myself off and got back in the kitchen. There were tears, there was laughter and there was being so broke that dinner was a 17p pack of noodles. But more importantly, there was a sense of achievement I had never felt before. I was the only one standing in my way and it was time to step aside.

I'm so glad I stuck to it. It wasn't easy and there were bad days and bad weeks of course, some worse than the ones that led me to the park in the first place. But good days too, and fantastic days, and spectacular days and days when I felt like the luckiest girl in the world. Joys which I would have never experienced if I quit when it felt like everything was against me.

All of it is made worthwhile when the customer comes to collect their cake and is delighted. Seeing the customer's face made it great for me. Seeing how happy I had made someone, doing something I love.

When you want to quit, when you feel like you can't do it and you want to walk away, stick with it, I promise it gets better.

But, if ultimately you decide it's not for you, there is no shame in that whatsoever. You must do what makes you happy.

If the tragedies that I went through before I started baking have taught me anything it's that life is too short. Too short to wonder what if. Too short to be stuck doing something you dislike. Too short to be anything but happy. Take control of your own life and your own happiness, whatever route that takes you down; with an apron on, or without.

It may sound like throughout this book, I've been putting you off or trying to scare you away from taking up this cake decorating career. I'm not. What I am doing however, is giving you the realities behind the apron that I never knew. Elements of the job I wish I knew when I had started. It wouldn't have stopped me but it certainly would have helped me.

You can't enter this half-heartedly. You need to throw your all into it for it to work.

You can do it. I believe in you.

Best of luck, and happy baking!

Britt xo

Meet Britt

Britt Whyatt, also known as She Who Bakes, lives in Kent and is a multi-award-winning blogger, baker, content creation consultant, public speaker and mental health advocate.

In 2010 after recovering from surgery and suffering badly from depression and anxiety after a string of family tragedies, Britt was tasked to bake a cake for a charity bake sale. Having never baked before she armed herself with a packet mix and a bowl and hoped for the best. Using her blogging background, she created a baking blog called She Who Bakes which became a very successful baking business from home.

Baking hundreds of cakes over the years for special occasions, Britt knows what it takes to make a home cake business flourish. Her successful blog has over 300,000 followers and she has a strong social media presence.

Amongst her many awards and accolades the most recent include: -

Kent Independent Traders Home Based Business of the Year Winner 2015. Kent Digital Awards Best Blog Gold Award Winner 2015. Kent Digital Awards Best Website: Lifestyle & Culture Bronze Award Winner 2015. Kent Women in Business Home Based Business of the Year Winner 2015.

Kent Independent Traders Home Based Business of the Year Winner 2016: Kent Independent Traders Entrepreneur of the Year Runner Up 2016: Kent Digital Awards Best Blog: Business Bronze Award Winner 2016: SME Awards Social Media Pioneer of the Year Finalist 2016: Kent Women In Business Home Based Business Woman of the Year Runner Up 2016.

UK Blog Awards Food & Drink Highly Commended 2017:

More about Britt can be found on her website
SheWhoBakes.co.uk

Templates

The following examples can either be copied, or to get copies of these as a PDF that can be directly printed these can be downloaded from:

https://hypnoarts.com/cakes-bakes-business

Contract Terms & Conditions Template

Customer Name: _____

Customer Address:_____

Contact telephone number: _____

Delivery Address:_____

Occasion: _____

Cake Details

Size of Cake: _____

Number of Servings: _____

Toppers/Decorations:_____

Cake Colours/Themes:_____

Cake Flavour(s):_____

Cake Filling Flavour(s):_____

Cake Stand:_____

Cake Description:_____

Notes/Sketches:

Cake Price: _____

Delivery Costs: _____

Total Due: _____

Deposit Paid: _____

Full Payment due by: _____

Date Ordered: ____/____/_____

Delivery Date: ____/____/_____

This is an agreement between _____
(hereafter referred to as "Cake Customer")

And _____ (hereafter
referred to as "Cake Decorator").

As your Cake Decorator, I agree to deliver the above mentioned cake in a timely and mutually agreed upon manner. Contingent on the following conditions:

1. A deposit of 50% is required to confirm order and contract for the above described services. The remaining balance will be due two weeks before the delivery date. Any changes to this order must be made at least two weeks prior to delivery/collection.

2. Deposits are non-refundable and non-transferable.

3. If the cake is collected, it is the Cake Customer's responsibility to ensure the safety of the cake until it's required destination. The Cake Decorator cannot be held liable for any damage to the cake after it has been collected.

4. If fresh flowers will be used on the cake it is the responsibility of the florist to determine flower safety and safe food practices and not the cake decorator.

5. It is the responsibility of the Cake Customer advise the Cake Decorator of any known allergies to any ingredients that may be used in the cakes. Cake ingredients or machinery may come in contact with nuts, milk, and wheat products. Allergen information is provided with all orders.

6. In the very unlikely event of severe medical, natural, or other emergencies, it may be necessary to retain an alternative Cake Decorator. We will make every effort to secure a replacement cake designer. If such a situation should occur and a suitable replacement is not found, responsibility and liability is limited to the return of all payments received for the event.

7. The Cake Customer agrees that there will be no order changes to the cake request prior to two weeks before the delivery date.

In agreement to the above mentioned terms the Client and a representative of The Cake Decorator sign below:

_____

Date_____

Signature of the Client

_____

Date_____

Signature of The Cake Decorator

Cake Disclaimer Template

By signing this form I can confirm my cake was collected / delivered in good condition to my specifications. It is now my responsibility to ensure the safety of the cake until it's required destination. The Cake Decorator cannot be held liable for any damage to the cake after it has been collected / delivered.

_____ Date_____

Signature of customer/venue representative

Other Information

Do not store decorated cakes in the fridge. If the cake is not being displayed immediately, leave in a cool, dry room inside the box.

We recommend cutting the cake in a grid pattern to achieve 2" x 1" square 'party portions'.

Once your cake has been cut it will last 3-4 days after your event.

Any allergens in your cake will be clearly labelled on the box. Please check these carefully.

If you have ordered a tiered cake, please be aware there will be a thin cake board between the tiers and wooden or plastic dowelling rods in the bottom tiers for support. These should be removed before cutting. Once you separate the tiers, you will see them sticking out of the cake and can be easily removed.

Please ensure all non-edible decorations are removed from the cake before serving.

Items to be removed

Cake Pricing Template

Example is for a 7" round vanilla birthday cake with jam and buttercream, covered in sugar-paste and topped with a modelled figure. Prices taken from Sainsbury's and Cake Craft World and are correct as of January 2016.

Ingredients/ Equipment	Cost Per Unit	Quantity (7" round example)	Exact Cost (7" round example)
Self Raising Flour	£1.40/kg	200g	£0.28
Caster Sugar	£1.80/kg	200g	£0.36
Unsalted Butter	£3.40/kg	200g	£0.68
Eggs	£2.40/12	4	£0.80
Plain Flour	£1.40/kg	50g	£0.07
Vanilla	£6.00/118ml	10ml	£0.51
Butter (for buttercream)	£3.40/kg	100g	£0.34
Icing Sugar	£1.60/kg	350g	£0.57
Seedless Jam	£0.75/454g	100g	£0.17
7" Thin Board	£0.62	1	£0.62

Ingredients/ Equipment	Cost Per Unit	Quantity (7" round example)	Exact Cost (7" round example)
10" round cake drum	£1.39	1	£1.39
10" box	£0.87	1	£0.87
1 meter 25mm ribbon	£0.56	1	£0.56
1 meter 15mm ribbon	£0.52	1	£0.52
Sugar paste	£4.20/kg	1kg	£4.20
Modelling paste	£2.50/250g	250g	£2.50
Pink Food colouring	£2.40	1	£2.40
Royal Icing	£1.10/500g	100g	£0.22
Greasproof paper	£2.25	1 meter	£0.23
Total Costs			GBP 17.29

Baking Time: 1 hour 30 minutes.
Decorating Time total: 6 hours.
Working at £5 per hour.
Cake cost:
time + ingredients/equipment
= **£54.79**. Rounded up to **£55.**

Accounts Template

Money Out

Date	Company	Amount	Payment	Referenc
1/12	Wilko	£10.55	Card	INV001
2/12	Sainsbury	£32.20	Card	INV002
2/12	Iced Jems	£25.70	Card	INV003
2/12	Poundland	£8.00	Cash	INV004

Money In

Date	Product	Amount	Payment	Receipt No
6/4	Cake C.Name	£150	BACS	21
7/4	Cupcakes J.Name	£40	Cash	22
13/4	Cake Deposit	£25	Paypal	23
17/4	Cake A.Name	£75	Cash	24

HypnoArts Publications

Enhancing the Experience of Life
and Boost Business

For the most up to date information on;
Books, Audio, Courses and Video Tutorials, Author
information, links to forums and FaceBook groups Live Author
Appearances and events download the free
#HypnoArts App
From iTunes App Store or Google Play or Visit:
HypnoArts.com and grab your copy of our
email newsletter.

We look forward to meeting you.

Jane Bregazzi. CEO HypnoArts